Let Us
Give Thanks

Also by Becca Anderson

New Beginnings
The Woman's Book of Prayer
Prayers for Calm
Prayers for Hard Times
Every Day Thankful
You Are an Awesome Woman

Let Us Give Thanks

Graces, Blessings and Prayers
for the Daily Meal

Becca Anderson

CORAL GABLES

For permission requests, please contact the publisher at:
Mango Publishing Group
2850 S Douglas Road, 4th Floor
Coral Gables, FL 33134 USA
info@mango.bz

For special orders, quantity sales, course adoptions and corporate sales, please email the publisher at sales@mango.bz. For trade and wholesale sales, please contact Ingram Publisher Services at customer.service@ingramcontent.com or +1.800.509.4887.

Let Us Give Thanks: Graces, Blessings and Prayers for the Daily Meal

Library of Congress Cataloging-in-Publication number: 2021945002
ISBN: (p) 978-1-64250-758-4 (e) 978-1-64250-759-1
BISAC category code OCC019000, BODY, MIND & SPIRIT / Inspiration & Personal Growth

Printed in the United States of America.

TABLE OF CONTENTS

FOREWORD

Close your eyes and think about the expression, "giving thanks." Does it bring to mind a Norman Rockwell painting depicting a family with bowed heads and clasped hands? Or do you think about the active, acknowledging a gift or act of kindness? This book aims to take you through those expressions of thankfulness and into the realm of transformative change, because seeing grace is a key ingredient in living a life full of joy and abundance.

I wasn't raised in a household that said grace, but I was keenly aware from a young age that I had much to be grateful for. Much later, after various travails severely tested that optimism and faith, I began searching for methods, practices, and tools to help me achieve a state of serenity and acceptance. What I discovered led to the writing of *Living Life as a Thank You*, which I coauthored with Mary Beth Sammons. As it turns out, there is no magic formula or one true spiritual path to discovering what gives life meaning. All it takes is two words—*thank you*—to profoundly change your outlook, and even your life.

No matter your relationship to organized religion, you can add this one ritual to your life. It will not only increase your appreciation of your food—it will increase the happiness quotient of those you dine with! Research from Harvard Medical School and other institutions shows that happiness is contagious. Happiness—and achieving a state of grace—is not something that you can purchase, wear, or travel to. It is a spiritual experience. And giving thanks is the one true path to happiness.

Many news and magazine articles continue to focus on the importance of the shared meal. It is often the only time we connect with other people who all live busy, full lives. Beyond that, we live in times when it seems like virtually everyone's meal with a shared prayer requires your table mates to turn their attention from fair-flung social networks to the bounty in front of them. What a blessing to have a vehicle that enables us to reconnect with our good fortune and those around us! In *Let Us Give Thanks*, we talk about how living a grateful life doesn't come naturally to many people. We need to work intentionally to increase the intensity, duration, and frequency of positive, grateful feelings. This book contains the tools to help you do that with very little effort, and a lot of pay off.

Who wouldn't want to promote health, harmony, peace, forgiveness, and empowerment in their lives and the lives of their loved ones? Saying thank you before a meal can help you capture those blessings. And with regular practice, expressing appreciation can bring abundance and greater love into your life. As Sri Ramakrishna Paramahamsa said, "The winds of grace blow all the time. All we need to do is set our sails."

—Nina Lesowitz

INTRODUCTION

I come from humble circumstances, and for this I am grateful. Many extended family lived on nearby farms in our civilian part of West Virginia, so there were always aunts and uncles and cousins stopping by with an extra bushel of corn or some freshly canned tomatoes for a sit-down and a nice, long "chin wag." It may have been my great-aunts and uncles, however, who most influence my childhood mind. To the survivors of the great war and the great depression, even modern conveniences such as ready baked bread you could buy in a store where the stuff of amazement. They had to grow their own food, bake their own bread, make their own clothes. They were DIY when it was not fashionable but essential.

Aunt Stella and Ida and Uncle Arthur were up with the sun milking cows and tending vegetable patches. Whatever needed doing to keep food on the table and a roof over their heads they did, and happily. I can imagine my Uncle Delbert's roaring laughter that butchery is now a trendy new hobby undertaken by hipsters in Brooklyn, Portland, San Francisco, and other foodie meccas. I had to help with the sausage-making and I have to agree with my forebears—butchering your own livestock is not glamorous (especially when some were your four-legged farm friends)!

I do think my aunties and uncles would appreciate the recent return to "the homely arts," and not because of my cultural zeitgeist but for this simple reason—what you make with your own hands, you'll appreciate more.

You see, they were grateful for the little things in life—nice weather, good health, and abundant harvest. I feel a sense of pride that my family also did a lot of "inner work" and we're fairly accomplished. Aunt Stella was a great dancer and made lace the Etsy crowd would go crazy for. Uncle Wilbur was a theologian and great orator—people would come from miles around to hear him preach. Pretty much everybody played piano or organ, and all were avid readers, so when I started reading and never stopped I even managed to escape a few chores this way—by disappearing inside a book and becoming oblivious to all else.

My elders also said grace at every meal over food they had grown and cooked themselves, sometimes adding a poetic or biblical quote to the mealtime prayer. I learned to be thankful back then on the farm by listening to stories of hard times when folks did without, a rather stoic all-purpose phrase these Depression-era veterans employed to encompass the lack of food, very little food, no new clothes or shoes, and only hand-me-downs. When I think back to those stories, which seemed mythological to me, they were not complaining. Instead, my elderly relatives related those stories with humor and, surprisingly, gratitude.

I am writing this on Thanksgiving Day, after enjoying a bountiful meal shared with cherished loved ones. And for that, I am filled with gratitude.

I also learned from my dear mother Helen that you only get what you give. I remember well her tithing even when we were having hard times. She would not hear of skipping a week, and I witnessed her do without new things for herself. So, I too will share some of the proceeds from this book to those who might be in need of a helping hand.

A portion of the proceeds from *Let Us Give Thanks* will be going to Building Opportunities for Selves-Sufficiency (BOSS). BOSS operates in network of housing and support services in Berkeley, Hayward, and Oakland, California, working directly with at-risk youth and families to help them get back on their feet. Their program provides whatever level of support people need and request in order to build health, wellness, and self-sufficiency, whether they're seeking one-time assistance or help for longer periods of time.

You can donate to BOSS via their website (www.self-sufficiency.org), or by mailing a check made out to BOSS to 22065 Kittredge St. Ste. E. Berkeley, CA, 94704. All donations are tax deductible.

With true gratitude,

—Becca Anderson

Opening to Gratitude

"In times of great stress or adversity, it's always best to keep busy, to plow your energy into something positive."
—Lee Iacocca

"I think I learned to appreciate and treasure each day, because you don't know how many you're going to be given."
—Sandra Day O'Connor

"We have all a better guide in ourselves, if we would attend to it, than any other person can be."
—Jane Austen

"No metaphysician ever felt the deficiency of language so much as the grateful."
—C.C. Colton

"Whatever I am offered in devotion with a pure heart—a leaf, a flower, fruit, or water—I accept with joy."
—The Bhagavad Gita

1 | Embrace This Day

I arise this day
With love in my heart,
Through the warmth of the sun,
The radiance of the moon,
Freedom of the win,
Joy of rushing water come
Splendor of fire,
Stability of earth,
Serenity of stars, and
The wisdom of silence.
I embrace this day
Through the grace of life to guide me
And the promise of love to inspire me.
—**Irish prayer**

2 | It Calls to You

It's not the day on the
calendar that makes the
New Year new, it's when
the old year dies that the new
year gets born. It's when the
ache in your heart breaks
open, when new love makes
every cell in your body
align. It's when your baby
is born, it's when your
father and mother die. It's
when the new Earth is

discovered and it's the
ground you're standing on.
The old year is all that is
broken, the ash left from all
those other fires you made;
the new year kindles from
your own spark, catches flame
and consumes all within
that is old, withered and dry.
The New Year breaks out
when the eye sees anew,
when the heart breathes open
locked rooms, when your
dead branches burst into
blossom, when the Call comes
with no doubt that it's calling to you.
—**Richard Wehrman**

The Lord's Gift | 3

To all else thou hast given us, O Lord,
we ask for but one thing more:
Give us
grateful hearts.
—**George Herbert**

4 | Hope for Healing and Love

Hardship often plays a significant role in birthing gratitude. There is a tension between wallowing in self-pity and turning that energy into tools of giving and gratitude-the whole glass half-full concept.

When brokenness and suffering enter our lives, we have a choice whether to let them simmer and stew, depleting our sense of peace, faith, and hope for healing and love.

That is the time when we have to be purposeful about bringing fresh ideas and perspectives, along with a greater sense of possibility, in place of the weariness sinking into our broken places.
—**Mary Beth Sammons**

5 | Simple Blessings

I am grateful for my family and friends, a job to earn my keep, and the health to do it, and opportunities and the lessons I've learned. Let me never lose sight of the simple blessings that form the fabric and foundation of my life. I am blessed, yesterday, today and tomorrow.
—**Abby Willowroot**

6 | Finding the Treasure Within

Looking behind,
I am filled with gratitude.

Looking forward,
I am filled with vision.
Looking upwards,
I am filled with strength.
Looking within,
I discover peace.
—**Native American Proverb**

Saying so Makes It So | 7

"Any day I'm vertical is a good day"
-that's what I always say.
And I give thanks
that I am healthy.
If you ask me,
"How are you?"
I'll answer, "GREAT!"
because in saying so,
I make it so.
And I give things
that I can choose my attitude.
When life gives me dark clouds and rain,
I appreciate the moisture
which brings a soft curl to my hair.
When Life gives me sunshine,
I gratefully turn my face up
to feel it warms on my cheeks.
When Life brings far,
I hug my sweater around me
and give thanks for the cool shroud of mystery
that makes the familiar seem different and intriguing.

When Life bring snow,
I dash outside to catch the first flakes on my tongue,
relishing the icy miracle that is a snowflake.
Life's events and experiences
are like the weather—
they come and go,
no matter what my preference.
So, what the heck?!
I might as well decide to enjoy them.
For indeed,
there IS a time for every purpose
under Heaven.
Each season brings its own unique blessings.
And I give thanks.
—BJ Gallagher

8 | How Much We've Been Given

Being thankful changes our energy from demanding to
appreciation. Instead of increasing our expectations of
how things should be, we can move toward recognizing
what is. I like learning from my pets—every caring
gesture or morsel of food is appreciated. It's important
to stay in touch with the reality of how much we've
been given.
—Dorothea Hover-Kramer

9 | New Mercies for Each Day

When trouble is close at hand.

Your Word will be a lamp for me,
a guide to light my way,
a solid place to set my feet,
a compass when I stray.

May I live my life to praise You,
not for fortune, nor for fame,
may everything I say and do
bring glory to Your name.

May my eyes stay fixed upon You
as I seek the way that's pure,
tasting Your love and goodness
sleeping and rising secure.

Planted by Your living streams
I'll delight in all Your ways,
hidden by Your sheltering wings
with new mercies for each day.

Even in a dangerous land
when storms threaten to destroy,
at the cross I'll stand upon the Rock
my Strength, my Hope, my Joy.

Dear Lord, show me Your favor,
at all times keep me blessed,
may Your face ever shine upon me,
with peace and perfect rest. Amen.
—**Mary Fairchild**

10 | Contentment as Is

He who knows that enough is enough
will always have enough.
—Lao Tzu

11 | It Takes a Second to Be Thankful

God gave you a gift of 86,400 seconds today.
Have you used one to say, "Thank you?"
—William A. Ward

12 | Be Thankful for the Difficult Times

Be thankful that you don't already have everything
you desire. If you did, what would there be to look
forward to?

Be thankful when you don't know something
For it gives you the opportunity to learn.

Be thankful for the difficult times.
During those times you grow.

Be thankful for your limitations
Because they give you opportunities for improvement.

Be thankful for each new challenge
Because it will build your strength and character.

Be thankful for your mistakes
They will teach you valuable lessons.

Be thankful when you're tired and weary
Because it means you've made a difference.

It is easy to be thankful for good things.
A life of rich fulfillment comes to those who are also
thankful for the setbacks.

Gratitude can turn a negative into a positive.

Find a way to be thankful for your troubles and they can
become your blessings.
—**Author Unknown**

Beauty of the Sun and the Soil | 13

So often bread is taken for granted,
Yet there is so much of beauty and bread-
Beauty of the sun and the soil,
Beauty of human soil.
Winds and rains have caressed it,
Christ, Himself, blessed it.
—**Christian prayer**

Serenity Prayer | 14

Living one day at a time;
enjoying one moment at a time;

accepting hardship as the pathway to peace.
Taking, as He did,
this sinful world as it is,
not as I would have it;
trusting that He will make all things right if
I surrender to His will;
that I may be reasonably happy in this life
and supremely happy with Him forever in the
next. Amen.
—**William Hutchison Murray**

15 | Friendsgiving

I awoke this morning with devout thanksgiving
for my friends, the old and the new.
—**Ralph Waldo Emerson**

16 | Seek and Ye Shall Find

Ask, and it shall be given you;
Seek, and you shall find;
Knock, and it shall be opened to you.
For whoever asks, receives;
And he who seeks, finds;
And to him who knocks, the door is opened.
—**Matthew 7:7, The Words of Christ**

I've Been to the Mountaintop | 17

Well, I don't know what will happen now.
We've got some difficult days ahead.
But it doesn't matter with me now.
Because I've been to the mountaintop.
And I don't mind.
Like anybody, I would like to live a long life.
Longevity has its place.
But I'm not concerned about that now.
I just want to do God's will.
And He's allowed me to go up to the mountain.
And I've looked over.
And I've seen the promised land.
I may not get there with you.
But I want you to know tonight, that we,
as a people will get to the promised land.
And I'm happy, tonight.
I'm not worried about anything.
I'm not fearing any man.
Mine eyes have seen the glory of the coming of the Lord.
—**Dr. Martin Luther King Jr.**

The Seven Steps to Effective Prayer | 18

1.

I release all of my past, negatives,
fears, human relationships, self-image, future,
and human desires to the Light.

2.
I am a Light Being.

3.
I radiate the Light from my Light Center
throughout my being.

4.
I radiate the Light
from my Light Center to everyone.

5.
I radiate the Light
from my Light Center to everything.

6.
I am in a bubble of Light
and only Light can come to me
and only Light can be here.

7.
Thank you, God, for everyone, for everything and for me.
—**Jim Goure**

19 | Wonder and Appreciation

Problems do not seem as overwhelming when you take
a few moments to count your blessings and appreciate
what exists in your life. Emotionally, gratitude is the
equivalent of taking a deep breath and relaxing.

Research shows that people who actively practice appreciation and gratitude in their lives are happier. The expression of gratitude is a feeling, a sense of all, wonder, and appreciation for what you have and what is around you.

—Susyn Reeve

How Beautiful It Is | 20

Oh God
Help me
to believe
the truth about myself
no matter
how beautiful it is!

—Macrina Wiederkehr

Remembrance of All Good Things | 21

Gratitude is the memory of the heart.

—Jean Baptiste Massieu

Grateful to All Gods | 22

Both in good fiction and in life, you may not always get what you want, but you will probably get what you need. We should be grateful for these things.

—Neil Gaiman

23 | Thanksgiving Prayer

O God, when I have food, help me to remember the
hungry. When I have work, help me to remember the
jobless. When I have a home, help me to remember
those who have no home at all. When I am without
pain, help me to remember those who suffer. And
remembering, help me to destroy my complacency, bestir
my compassion, and be concerned enough to help, by
word and deed, those who cry out for what we take for
granted. Amen.
—**Samuel F. Pugh**

24 | Share All Your Honey

Piglet noticed that even though he had a Very Small
Heart, it could hold a rather large amount of Gratitude.
—**A. A. Milne**

25 | Inspire Me to Kindness, Each and Every Day

Day by day,
Let me see the grace
Day by day,
Let me see the way

Day by day,
Let me see the beauty
Let me hear the music

day by day
Let me see the way

Day by day
let me see the goodness
Let me feel the love
Inspire me to kindness
Day by day,
let me see the way

Let me see the grace
Let me see the way
Day by Day
—Hans van Rostenberghe

Gratitude, Humility, & Understanding | 26

"Thank you" is the best prayer that anyone could say.
I say that one a lot. Thank you expresses extreme
gratitude, humility, and understanding.
—Alice Walker

The Zen of Thankfulness | 27

In our daily lives, we must see that it is not happiness
that makes us grateful, but the gratefulness that
makes us happy.
—Albert Clarke

28 | Teach Grace

The Great Spirit is in all things. He is in the air we breathe. The Great Spirit is our Father, but the Earth is our Mother. She nourishes us... That which we put into the ground she returns to us.

—**Big Thunder Wabanaki, Algonquin**

29 | Giving Thanks for the Mystery of It All

To be grateful means giving thanks for more than just the things we want, but also for the things that surmount our pride and stubbornness...

Sometimes just giving thanks for the mystery of it all brings everything and everyone closer, the way suction full streams of water together. So, take a chance and openly give thanks, even if you're not sure what for, and feel the pressure to Dove all that is living brush up against your heart.

—**Mark Nepo**

30 | Food for the Soul

Salutations!
O Merciful God
Who provides food for the body and soul,
You who have kindly granted what is spread before us.
We thank you.

Bless the loving hands that prepared this meal and us
who are to enjoy it, please.
Homage, homage,
Homage to thee!
—**Tamil Prayer**

Never Be Less | 31

May the abundance of this table
Never fail and never be less,
Thanks to the blessings of God,
Who has satisfied our needs.
To Him be the glory forever. Amen.

In peace let us eat this food
Which the Lord hath provided for us.
Blessed be the Lord in His gifts. Amen.

Glory be to the father, and to the Son,
And to the Holy Ghost, now and always,
World without end. Amen.
—**Armenian Grace**

A Thankful Heart

"I am grateful for what I am and have. My thanksgiving is perpetual."
—**Henry David Thoreau**

"The struggle ends when gratitude begins."
—**Neale Donald Walsch**

" 'Enough' is a feast."
—**Buddhist Proverb**

"Wake at dawn with a winged / Heart and give thanks for / Another day of loving."
—**Khalil Gibran**

"Let us be grateful to the people who make us happy; they are the charming gardeners who make our souls blossom."
—**Marcel Proust**

"It is impossible to feel grateful and depressed in the same moment."
—**Naomi Williams**

All We Need Is Love | 1

I will not wait to love as best as I can. We thought we
were young and that there would be time to love well
sometime in the future. This is a terrible way to think. It
is no way to live, to wait to love.
—Dave Eggers

One More Hour to Love | 2

One more day to serve.
One more hour to love.
One more minute to praise.
For this day I am grateful.
If I awaken to the morning sun,
I am grateful.
—Mary Lou Kownacki

Life's Riches | 3

In ordinary life, we hardly realize that we receive a good
deal more than we give, and that it is only with gratitude
that life becomes rich.
—Dietrich Bonhoeffer

Tasting the Tigris in Every Sip | 4

Even a prayer, our eyes look inward;
If the gate to the holy is shut, we just turn away.

The One is only the One, everyone knows–
What mirroring icon could hold it face-to-face?

Held back unnoticed, grief bruises the heart;
Not reaching the river, a raindrop is swallowed by dust.

If a story brings only tears and not blood to the eyes,
It is only a lovers' tale.

Whoever can't see the whole in every part play at blind
man's bluff;
A wise man tastes the Tigris in every sip.
—Ghalib

5 | The Energy of Gratitude

Focusing on one thing that you are grateful for increases
the energy of gratitude and rises the joy inside yourself.
—Oprah Winfrey

6 | Be Here Now

No longer forward nor behind
I look in hope or fear;
But, grateful, take the good I find,
The best of now and here.
—John Greenleaf Whittier

Gifts of the Heart | 7

Kindness is a hard thing to give away;
it keeps coming back to the giver.
—**Ralph Scott**

Blessing to Blessing | 8

Learn to get in touch with the silence within yourself
and know that everything has a purpose. There are no
mistakes, no coincidences, all events are blessings giving
to us to learn from.
—**Elisabeth Kübler-Ross**

Satisfaction Guaranteed | 9

It is wealth to be content.
—**Lao Tzu**

Blessed Be | 10

Blessed are those who give without remembering.
And blessed are those who take without forgetting.
—**Bernard Meltzer**

11 | All We Have Is Now

We have only this moment, sparkling like a star in our hand...and melting like a snowflake. Let us use it now before it is too late.
—**Marie Beynon Lyons Ray**

12 | Thresholds of Gratitude

Gratitude opens the door, the power, the wisdom, the creativity of the universe. You open the door through gratitude.
—**Deepak Chopra**

13 | I Love You, I Thank You

Aloha to God above,
Aloha, a word that means
I love you.
Mahalo too, means
I thank you.
Mahalo, aloha to God.
—**Hawaiian Grace**

Love, Grace, & Gratitude | 14

Happiness cannot be traveled to, owned, earned, worn or consumed. Happiness is a spiritual experience of living every minute with love, grace and gratitude.
—Denis Waitley

Universal Truth | 15

Nothing behind me, everything ahead of me, as is ever so on the road.
—Jack Kerouac, ON THE ROAD

For Everything Thy Goodness Sends | 16

For each new morning with its light, for rest and shelter of the night, for health and food, for love and friends, for everything Thy goodness sends.
—Ralph Waldo Emerson

We Are Roses | 17

We wouldn't ask why a rose that grew from the concrete has damaged petals; in turn, we would all celebrate its tenacity, we would all love its will to reach the sun. Well, we are the roses: this is the concrete and these are my damaged petals, don't ask me why. Thank God and ask me how.
—Tupac Shakur

18 | God Adores His Creations

I think God might be a little prejudiced.
For once He asked me to join Him on a walk
through this world,
and we gazed into every heart on this earth,
and I noticed He lingered a bit longer
before any face that was weeping,
and before any eyes that were laughing.
And sometimes when we passed
a soul in worship
God too would kneel down.
I have come to learn:
God adores His creation.
—**St. Francis of Assisi**

19 | Amazing Grace

Amazing grace! How sweet the sound
That saved a wretch like me.
I once was lost, but now am found,
Was blind, but now I see.
'Twas grace that taught my heart to fear,
And grace my fears were relieved.
How precious did that grace appear
The hour I first believed.
Through many dangers, toils and snares
I have already come;
'Tis grace hath brought me safe thus far
And grace will lead me home.
The Lord has promised good to me

His word my hope secures;
He will my shield and portion be,
As long as life endures.
Yea, when this flesh and heart shall fail,
and mortal life shall cease,
I shall possess within the veil,
A life of joy and peace.
When we've been there ten thousand years
Bright shining as the sun,
We've no less days to sing God's praise
Than when we've first begun.
—**John Newton**

Showing Appreciation | 20

Make it a habit to tell people thank you. To express your
appreciation, sincerely and without the expectation of
anything in return. Truly appreciate those around you,
and you'll soon find many others around you. Truly
appreciate life, and you'll find that you have more of it.
—**Ralph Marston**

Unexpected Blessings | 21

When we lose one blessing, another is often most
unexpectedly given in its place.
—**C.S. Lewis**

22 | The Time of Our Lives

Dreaming of the person you want to be
is wasting the person you already are.
—**Kurt Donald Cobain**

23 | Gifts from God

Start living now. Stop saving the good China for that
special occasion. Stop withholding your love until that
special person materializes. Every day you are alive
as a special occasion. Every minute, every breath, is a
gift from God.
—**Mary Manin Morrissey**

24 | The Visiting Stranger

Dear and beloved stranger, please eat this food with us so
that we may all be nourished. Please share this walk with
us that we may all know nature's peace. Please rest in this
warm house so that we may come to know each other.
Please sleep under these soft blankets so that we may all
know safety. Please pray this prayer so that all our names
of God may guide us on.
—**Christina Baldwin**

The Interconnectedness of All Life | 25

I do not think the measure of a civilization is how tall
its buildings of concrete are, but rather how well its
people have learned to relate to their environment and
fellow man.
—Sun Bear, Chippewa

Gifts Come in Many Forms | 26

After a good dinner one can forgive anybody,
even one's own relations.
—Oscar Wilde

Try Again and Again to Make Peace | 27

Great God, who has told us
"Vengeance is mine,"
save us from ourselves,
save us from the vengeance in our hearts
and the acid in our souls.

Save us from our desire to hurt as we have been hurt,
to punish as we have been punished,
to terrorize as we have been terrorized.

Give us the strength it takes
to listen rather than to judge,
to trust rather than to fear,
to try again and again
to make peace even when peace eludes us.

We ask, O God, for the grace
to be our best selves.
We ask for the vision
to be builders of the human community
rather than its destroyers.
We ask for the humility as a people
to understand the fears and hopes of other peoples.

We ask for the love it takes
to bequeath to the children of the world to come
more than the failures of our own making.
We ask for the heart it takes...

Amen.
—Sister Joan Chittister

28 | Sacred Grove of Eternity

The garden is rich with diversity
With plants of a hundred families
In the space between the trees
With all the colors and fragrances
Basil, mint, and lavender,
God keep my remembrance pure,
Raspberry, Apple, Rose,

God fill my heart with love,
Dill, anise, tansy,
Holy winds blow in me.
Rhododendron, zinnia,
May my prayer be beautiful
May my remembrance O God
Be an incense to thee
In the sacred grove of eternity
As I smell and remember
The ancient forest of earth.
—**Chinook Psalter**

The Meaning of Life | 29

I had this thought that the only thing that God requires
from us is to enjoy life and love. It doesn't matter if you
accomplish anything. You don't have to do anything but
appreciate that you're alive—and love. That's the whole
point... You like to make music? Fine, go ahead. Make
sure that if you do that, what people get from it is joy.
—**Paul Simon**

Renewing Grace

"He that is hard to please may get nothing in the end."
—**Aesop**

"Gratitude is not only the greatest of virtues, but the parent of all others."
—**Cicero**

"You don't have to be anything but yourself to be worthy."
—**Tarana Burke**

"Joy is the simplest form of gratitude."
—**Karl Barth**

"You are enough. You are so enough. It is unbelievable how enough you are."
—**Sierra Boggess**

"Take full account of what Excellencies you possess, and in gratitude remember how you would hanker after them, if you had them not."
—**Marcus Aurelius**

Oneness, the Universe, and All Its Powers | 1

What is Life? It is the flash of a firefly in the night. It is the breath of a buffalo in the wintertime. It is the little shadow which runs across the grass and loses itself in the sunset. The True Peace. The first peace, which is the most important, is that which comes within the souls of people when they realize their relationship, their oneness, with the universe and all its powers, and when they realize that at the center of the universe dwells Wakan-Taka (the Great Spirit), and that this center is really everywhere, it is within each of us. This is the real peace, and the others are but reflections of this. The second peace is that which is made between two individuals, and the third is that which is made between two nations. But above all you should understand that there can never be peace between nations until there is known that true peace, which, as I have often said, is within the souls of men.
—**Black Elk, Oglala Sioux and Spiritual Leader**

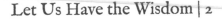

Let Us Have the Wisdom | 2

May there be food for all
Let us give thanks
For the food we are about to eat.
May there be food for all,
Abundant and healthful.
Let us have the wisdom to choose to eat only that
Which enhances our precious energy

And sustains us through our labors and rest.
—**Adapted from A Haggadah of Liberation**

3 | Do the Math

The hardest arithmetic to master
is that which enables us to count our blessings.
—**Eric Hoffer**

4 | Thinking of Others

Reframe your thoughts on giving. When we think of "giving." When we think of giving, we often think of donating money to a cause. We can give numerous other gifts, such as our time, our presence, and our caring
—**Nina Lesowitz**

5 | We Are on the Same Path

Religions are different roads
converging upon the same point.
What does it matter
that we take different roads
so long as we reach the same goal.
—**Mahatma Gandhi**

Kabbalah in Hebrew means "to accept." Kabbalah teaches us how to flow with God's work by accepting it. The oyster holds the same secrets; it teaches us to accept our weaknesses and disabilities. We are perfect in our imperfections; that is the secret paradox of life. What makes us perfect is the ability to grow, and we can only grow if we are not yet perfect. As long as we have some imperfections, we are participating in God's creation. That is the key of life and that is the Jewel in the Lotus. We often spent too much time in gratitude for what is going well in our life, but as God is One, the perfect and imperfect and you are also one. Spend some time focusing on showing your gratitude toward the imperfections that make you so perfect.
—Gahl Sasson

Never Give Up | 7

As I look around,
I see the crumbling ruins of civilization
like a vast heap of futility.

Yet I shall not commit
the grievous sin
of losing faith in man.
—**Rabindranath Tagore**

8 | May All Women Be Respected by Men

Great Spirit, I am Mother.
I was made by You
So that the image of Your love
Could be brought into existence.
May I always carry with me
The sacredness of this honor.

Creator, I am Daughter.
I am the learner of the Traditions.
May I carry them forward
So that the Elders and Ancestors
Will be remembered for all time.

Maker-of-All-Things, I am Sister.
Through me, may my brothers be shown
The manner in which I am to be respected.
May I join with my sisters in strength
And power as a Healing Shield
So that they will no longer bear
The stain of abuse.

Niskam, I am
Committed Partner: One who shares her spirit,
But is wise to remember never to give it away,
Lest it become lost,
And the two become less than one.

I am Woman. Hear me. Welal'in. Ta'ho!
—**Native American Chant**

Open House | 9

This being human is a guest house.
Every morning a new arrival.

A joy, a depression, a meanness,
some momentary awareness comes
as an unexpected visitor.

Welcome and entertain them all!
Even if they're a crowd of sorrows,
who violently sweep your house
empty of its furniture,
still, treat each guest honorably.
He may be clearing you out
for some new delight.

The dark thought, the shame, the malice,
meet them at the door laughing,
and invite them in.

Be grateful for whoever comes,
because each has been sent
as a guide from beyond.
—**Rumi**

Stewards of the Earth | 10

We give thanks for the Sun even when
behind clouds it hides.
We give thanks for the Wind

though it bends the birches low.
We get thanks for Rain, gentle or torrential.
We give thanks for the Earth.
For its Beauty and Glory and Power we give thanks.
Give us grace to be good stewards of this our Inheritance.
—**Annabelle Woodard**

11 | The Soul of Nature That Gives Life to the Universe

Great Spirit, Divine One, Creator
who is heaven earth rock wind insect tree fox
human of every size shape color

Holy are your infinite names chanted sung whispered
shouted in every language, tongue.

We will midwife the rebirth of Gaia
as best we can
restoring the Great Law of Peace.

Guide our hands to the soil and seed
honoring the alchemy of food.
Let us remember your abundance
and share the bread of life with any who hunger.

We are for giving
and giving and giving.
We trust in the give-away.
We give and receive.

Let us be humble before the darkness and the light
walking in harmony amidst them.
Give us courage to know them intimately
both within and without.

For you have breathed it all—
the behind, the above, the below, the beyond.
Your awesome power courses in our veins
and animates our hearts.
You are the Great Drum.

We thank you.
—**Translation of the Lord's Prayer from King James to
Gaian, Claudia L'Amoreaux**

Gathering Strength | 12

Earth, when I am about to die, I lean upon you.
Earth, while I am alive, I depend upon you.
—**Prayer from Ashanti, Ghana**

You Are for Me a Mirror | 13

Mary, my Mother and my Lady,
I offer You my soul, my body,
my life and my death,
and all that will follow it.
I place everything in Your hands.
O my Mother, cover my soul
with Your virginal mantle

and grant me the grace of purity
of heart, soul, and body.
Defend me with Your power
against all enemies, and especially
against those who hide their malice
behind the mask of virtue.
O lovely lily!
You are for me a mirror,
O my Mother!
—St. Faustina

14 | Sparking the Inner Flame

Sometimes we feel deflated, or overwhelmed, or someone
or something hurts us, disappoints us, or we hear bad
news about a loved one's medical condition. And those
days, when you feel your light has gone out, remember
there is always a glimmer of hope and something to be
thankful for. Sometimes our light goes out but is blown
again into instant flame by an encounter with another
human being. Each of us shows the deepest things to
those who have rekindled this inner light.
—Albert Schweitzer

15 | Harbor in Good

I celebrate myself, and sing myself,
And what I assume you shall assume,
For every atom belonging to me as good belongs to you.

I loafe and invite my soul,
I lean and loafe at my ease observing a spear of
summer grass.

My tongue, every atom of my blood,
form'd from this soil, this air,
Born here of parents born here from parents the same,
and their parents the same,
I, now thirty-seven years old in perfect health begin,
Hoping to cease not till death.

Creeds and schools in abeyance,
Retiring back a while sufficed at what they are,
but never forgotten,
I harbor for good or bad,
I permit to speak at every hazard,
Nature without check with original energy.
—**Verse one of "Song of Myself," Walt Whitman**

What Small Thing Can You Do Today? | 16

In this life we cannot do great things.
We can only do small things with great love.
—**Mother Teresa**

17 | Recognizing the Unseen

To Muslims, prayer is a ladder, a journey reaching to heaven. St. Therese of Lisieux called it "an uplifting of the heart." In the words of William James, prayer is the soul and essence of religion," and to Auguste Sabatier, "religion in action." According to the Dakota Sioux physician and author, Ohiyesa, "In the Life of the Indian there was only one inevitable duty—the duty of prayer—the daily recognition of the Unseen and Eternal." Mahatma Gandhi practiced a "prayer that needs no speech," and Thomas Merton struggled for a form of prayer in everyday life "with everything I touch." For Brother David Steindl-Rast, "Prayer is unlimited mindfulness."
—Phil Cousineau

18 | Be a Candle

There are two ways of spreading light:
to be the candle or the mirror that reflects it.
—Edith Wharton

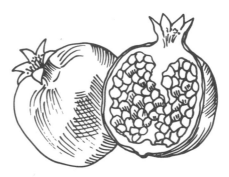

Because when death sits on your shoulder each day, whispering, urging you to your end, there is no time to lose, so much light to grasp before, strive for, struggle to embrace. We are struggling with life. And yet we are only human after all, so terribly flawed and foolish, selfish and ridiculous. Sobriety can be so messy. At times, I have seen to myself the most awful persons. But even then I am ascending, even then I am going up a ladder of light with eyes wide open and hands outstretched, to class the next rung up. And I climb.

—Alan Kaufman

Tear off the Paper, Look Inside | 20

When I can no longer say thank you
for this new day and the waking into it,
for the cold scrape of the kitchen chair
and the ticking of the space heater glowing
orange as it warms the floor near my feet,
I know it is because I've been fooled again
by the selfish, unruly man who lives in me
and believes he deserves only safety
and comfort. But if I pause as I do now,
and watch the streetlights outside winking
off one by one like old men closing their
cloudy eyes, if I listen to my tired neighbors
slamming car doors hard against the morning
and see the steaming coffee in their mugs
kissing their chapped lips as they sip and

exhale each of their worries white into
the icy air around their faces—then I can
remember this one life is a gift each of us
was handed and told to open: Untie the bow
and tear off the paper, look inside
and be grateful for whatever you find
even if it is only the scent of a tangerine
that lingers on the fingers long after
you've finished eating it.
—James Crews

21 | Lucky in Life

Property is for the comfort of life, not for the
accumulation of wealth. A sage, having been asked who
is lucky and who is not, replied: "He is lucky who has
eaten and sowed, but he is unlucky who has died and
not enjoyed."
—Sa'di

22 | On Earth as It Is in Heaven

God has two dwellings; one in heaven,
and the other in a meek and thankful heart.
—Isaak Walton

You Never Know | 23

Live with awareness. Be open to all of life, even when it's uncomfortable, unhappy, and imperfect. Uncomfortable moments can motivate us to take action that can result in meaningful experiences.
—**Polly Campbell**

Always Be Ready | 24

A problem is a chance for you to do your best.
—**Duke Ellington**

Help Me Now in My Urgent Need | 25

O Holy St. Jude!
Apostle and Martyr,
great in virtue and rich in miracles,
near kinsman of Jesus Christ,
faithful intercessor for all who invoke you,
special patron in time of need;
to you I have recourse from the depth of my heart,
and humbly beg you,
to whom God has given such great power,
to come to my assistance;
help me now in my urgent need
and grant my earnest petition.
I will never forget thy graces
and favors you obtain for me
and I will do my utmost to spread devotion to you.

Amen.

St. Jude, pray for us and all who honor thee and
invoke thy aid.

(Say three Our Fathers, three Hail Mary, and
three Glory Be)
—**Novena to St. Jude**

26 | As You Give as so Shall You Receive

Gratitude is the closest thing to beauty
manifested in an emotion.
—**Mindy Kaling**

27 | Ring Everything from Every Moment of Life

I will not die an unlived life.
I will not live in fear
of falling or catching fire.
I choose to inhabit my days,
to allow my living to open me,
to make me less afraid,
more accessible,
to loosen my heart
until it becomes a wing.
—**Dawna Markova**

Today I Purpose to Love

My life will shine
As the morning sings
I walk in liberty
Bound in true dreams
Manifested promises
Chase my forward motion
A covered path before me
The fruits of my hoping
The fruits of my living

Today I purpose to love

My love will speak
With the sound of grace
Merciful within mercy
The works of my faith
Smiles of overflowing
Inspire my giving
Abundance of joy as rain
The fruits of my living
—**Michael John Faciane**

29 | Serving Others

[I] focus on gratitude and being of service. It gets me
excited to want to take care of my guests, be it family,
friends, or a work-related function.
—**Antoni Porowski**

30 | Free Yourself with the Truth

You're not alone.
So long as you reach out to others you're never alone.
Ask for my help in loaning you
the courage you already have.
It's not that I never give you more than you can handle,
I am not responsible
for the consequences of your actions,
only you are. Stay on the path of your suffering
by taking the steps you need to take.
Hang on and hang in there, because it's now
that you're growing at light speed,
You're never going backward, only forward.
Decay your loneliness, by making full use
of my greatest gift to mankind, which is mankind.
Feel my alleged absence as proof,
for the paradox that I exist and have always existed.
Let me in by letting me out.
Love, fear, and all of the other feelings spared
are what create this reality.
These are the cause and effect of compassion and
true forgiveness.

Ask for my help in walking through the anguish
of forgiveness.
Do everything in your power to learn to forgive
and love those that hurt you,
Not for just them, but for others as well as yourself.
And never give up the hope that someday your
ex-suffering
will be able to help the ones who were sick and hurt you,
As well as those who suffered like you.
Learn all this by practicing to love everyone.
Always look into yourself first;
your past, your present, your motives,
your feelings, and share the secrets
you find with myself as well as others.
Be gentle and kind to yourself
by being vulnerable, and sharing yourself
with others who are patient, kind, and who can only
try to love and accept you as much as I do.
As you get better at this,
take the risks that will enable you to venture out
further and further, so that your true self
may finally be exposed to the real world
I created for you to live in.
Be honest with everyone by never
accepting the blame that is not yours.
Free yourself with the truth, by telling
those stepping on your toes how you feel,
no matter how difficult it may seem at first, or
what its consequences may be;
you'll only get better at it.
If you can learn to love, forgive,
fully listen, understand, and accept those around you,

you will eventually begin to learn how to love, forgive,
fully listen, understand, and accept yourself.
—**Author Unknown**

31 | By the Awful Grace of God

And even in our sleep,
pain that cannot forget
falls drop by drop upon the heart,
and in our own despite,
against our will,
comes wisdom to us
by the awful grace of God.
—**Agamemnon, Aeschylus, fifth century BCE**

The Season of New Beginning

"Prosperity is a great teacher; adversity is a greater."
—William Hazlitt

"When our perils are past, shall our gratitude sleep? No—
here's to the pilot that weathered the storm."
—George Canning

"I have found that worry and irritation vanish the
moment when I open my mind to the many blessings
that I possess"
—George Canning

"The smallest act of kindness is worth more than the
grandest intention."
—Oscar Wilde

"God may be in the details, but the goddess is in the
questions. Once we begin to ask them, there's no
turning back."
—Gloria Steinem

"Ingratitude is the most abominable of sins... For it is a
forgetting of the graces, benefits, and blessings received."
—St Ignatius Loyola

1 | Prayer for Calmness

God, grant me the serenity
To stop beating myself up for not doing things perfectly,
The courage to forgive myself
because I'm working on doing better,
And the wisdom to know that
You already love me just the way I am.
—**Eleanor Brownn**

2 | Compassion for All Who Suffer

Satveshu Maitrim Gunishu Pramodham
Klishteshu Jivehu Krupa Parathvam
Madhyastha Bhavam Viparita Vruthow
Sada Mamatma Viddhatu Deva

O Lord! Make myself such that
I may have love for all beings,
Joy in the meritorious,
unstinted sympathy for the distressed
And tolerance towards the perversely inclined.

O Lord! May my soul always find fulfillment, in
friendship and love towards all beings,
In all the virtuous, in compassion toward all
suffering creatures,
And in remaining neutral towards those hostile to me.
This is my prayer.
—**Ancient Jain Prayer of Love for All**

Unbelievably Golden | 3

For everything bad, there's a million really exciting
things, whether it's someone puts out a really great book,
there's a new movie, there's a new detective, the sky is
unbelievably golden, or you have the best cup of coffee
you ever had in your life.
—**Patti Smith**

Be Fully Present | 4

Live loyally today
—grow—
and tomorrow will attend to itself.
The quickest way for a tadpole to become a frog
is to live loyally each moment
as a tadpole.
—**The Urantia Book, 1094:06**

Planting Seeds | 5

All the flowers of all the tomorrows
are in the seeds of today.
—**Indian Proverb**

6 | Graciousness

Hospitality is all about graciously giving and taking. It's
not about impressing people or overcoming them with
your cleverness or skill. It's simply sharing what you
have and taking what is offered. The greatest hospitality
I've ever been shown was when I invited someone to my
house for dinner without knowing they were vegetarian.
They ate the food that was offered with nothing but a
heartfelt "thank you." And baby, it was ribs.
—**Alton Brown**

7 | Truth & Beauty

Life is full of beauty. Notice it. Noticed the bumblebee,
the small child, and smiling faces. Smell the rain and feel
the wind. Live your life to the fullest potential, and fight
for your dreams.
—**Ashley Smith**

8 | With Deep Prayer Comes Deep Peace

Pray for what you cannot see.
Pray clearly
for what you can only faintly grasp.
Pray silently
from the core of your being.
Pray for healing.
Pray for humanity.

Pray lovingly
Pray deeply—
pray so deeply that
the prayer and the praying
become one.
—**Charlie Elkind**

Sheer Joy | 9

When you rise in the morning,
Give thanks for the light, for your life, for your strength.
Give thanks for your food and for the joy of living.
If you see no reason to give thanks,
The fault lies in yourself.
—**Tecumseh**

Be Inspiring | 10

You never take life for granted. You never receive
possibilities lately. The opportunity is always there
to help somebody. We all need help remaining in
touch with our spirit and finding our own voice and
locating inspiration.
—**Alicia Keys**

11 | Listening to Stillness

Know how to live within yourself: there is in your soul a whole world of mysterious and in chanted thoughts; they will be drowned by the noise without; daylight will drive them away; listen to their singing and be silent.
—**Fyodor Tyutchev**

12 | Live Beautifully

Well, you're beautiful. Go out and live like it.
—**Bill Clinton**

13 | Prayer for Protection from All Danger

Circle me, Lord.
Keep protection near
And danger afar.
Circle me, Lord
Keep hope within.
Keep doubt without.
Circle me, Lord.
Keep light near
And darkness afar.
Circle me, Lord.
Keep peace within.
Keep evil out.
—**Coptic Christian Blessing**

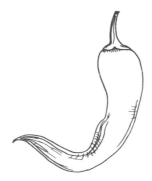

Appreciate Deeply | 14

Dear God, After the sadness I didn't think
I could ever be the same again.
I was right. I now have qualities
I never had before.
I am more sensitive to the sorrows of others.
I am more compassionate to the less fortunate.
I appreciate deeply.
I love more intensely.
Thank You for giving me the wisdom
that comes from life experiences.
Amen.
—**Martha Lynn, Harmony Hollows**

The Cathedral of Nature | 15

Look at nature. Nature is filled with wheat fields. Nature is filled with fruit trees. Nature is filled with all its gifts. It is abundant in every way. You are a willing receiver of these fruits, of these gifts. In return, is it too much to ask for you to give your blessings to the Earth Mother? She needs them. She needs them right now. Dance on her. Drum on her. Love on her. She needs you. She needs your love, your respect, your trust. She needs you to enjoy her. Give her lots of love, for she has been ignored to the nth degree. Your buildings—not one of them is as beautiful as one of her mountains. See with your eyes the beauty she has given to you; that she gives to you every single day. Give her love and attention and she will give

it back to you in countless ways, in ways that you can
barely imagine...
—Tony Burroughs

16 | All Blessings Flow

Praise God from whom all blessings flow;
praise him, all creatures here below;
praise him above, ye heavenly host:
Praise Father, Son, and Holy Ghost.
—**Traditional hymn, words by Thomas Ken**

17 | We Who Believe in Life Give Life

Hallelujah! They have risen!
Snowdrop, crocus, bearded iris.
Exult and throw your happy arms upward!
The trillium is carpeting the forest floor.
The tulips, triumphant and glorious
in rainbow rows,
rise up singing "our cups overflow."

The creatures dress in their feast-day finest,
the loons and penguins in black tie and tux.
Hallelujah ushers forth from lips and beaks
as quacks,
warbles, howls and hoots
fill the forests and fields with hymns of joy.

Let the Earth be glad and the sky shower praise

for the riot of color in her cloak of glory:

purple martin, scarlet tanager,
red-winged blackbird, yellow-bellied flycatcher,
great blue heron, snowy egret,
ruby-crowned kinglet, indigo bunting.

It is right to give thanks and to pray for the endangered,
relatives among us but not for long:

Bengal tiger, blue whale, leatherback sea turtle,
Asian elephant, Javan rhinoceros, mountain gorilla,
snow leopard, red wolf, California condor.

It is fitting that we mourn our relations now extinct-
though the list is long, let us name a few:

Chinese river dolphin, Japanese sea lion,
Caribbean monk seal,
Cascade mountain wolf, Sardinian lynx, Bali tiger,
Mexican grizzly, eastern cougar, black rhinoceros,
koala lemur,
Barbary lion, laughing owl.

For all that dies and rises, we bend our knee.

As creatures of the Cosmos, progeny of the Universe,
we give thanks and rejoice for the Flame within us.
With the bald eagles and hairy frogfish,
with the furry kittens and spiny hedgehogs,
with the runny-nosed bison and red-nosed reindeer
we stand in awe as Earth spins, tides change,

hearts beat, eyes see, hands comfort.

We who believe in Life give Life.
In adoration, we sing, we bow,
we weep tears of joy and tears of anguish.

This feast marks the life of a prophet
and teacher who said, more than once,
"What you see me do, you can do, and more."
That is what this praise is for.

What rises today and every new dawn
are these words that remind us:
There is nothing in the world we cannot do.

Let us rise, let us pray, let us sing.
Let us take this suffering world into our loving arms
and rock and rock and rock.

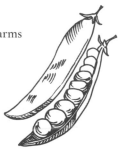

"Hallelujah! Hallelujah!
—"Easter Hymn for Earth," Jan Phillips

18 | Look Out Your Window

One of the most tragic things I know about human
nature is that all of us tend to put off living. We are all
dreaming of some magical rose garden over the horizon-
instead of enjoying the roses blooming outside our
windows today.
—Dale Carnegie

O Thou Who art generous and merciful!
We are the servants of Thy threshold and are gathered
beneath the sheltering shadow of Thy divine unity.
The sun of Thy mercy is shining upon all,
and the clouds of Thy bounty shower upon all.
Thy gifts encompass all,
Thy loving providence sustains all,
Thy protection overshadows all, and the glances of
Thy favor is cast upon all.
O Lord! Grant Thine infinite bestowals,
and let the light of Thy guidance shine.
Illumine the eyes, gladden the hearts with abiding joy.
Confer a new spirit upon all people and bestow upon
them eternal
life.

Unlock the gates of true understanding
and let the light of faith shine resplendent.
Gather all people beneath the shadow of Thy bounty
and cause them to unite in harmony,
so that they may become as the rays of one sun,
as the waves of one ocean, and as the fruit of one tree.
May they be refreshed by the same breeze.
May they receive illumination from the same
source of light.
Thou art the Giver, the Merciful, the Omnipotent.

—'Abdu'l-Bahá

20 | Abundance Is with Everyone

Let us pray for all to be happy,
to love one another,
to help each other,
to gain wisdom,
for all to receive god's blessings,
to break free from the illusion
that is distracting us from our true nature.

No one shall go hungry,
no one will suffer,
abundance is with everyone
and all negativity shall be removed!
—**Unitarian Universalist Blessing**

21 | A Rose Is a Rose Is a Rose

The roses under my window make no reference to
former roses or better ones; they are what they are;
they exist with God today. There is no time for them.
There is simply the rose; it is perfect in every moment of
its existence.
—**Ralph Waldo Emerson**

22 | Toward Heaven

If you cannot refuse to fall down,
refuse to stay down.
If you cannot refuse to stay down

lift your heart toward heaven
and like a hungry beggar,
ask that it be filled,
and it will be filled.
You may be pushed down.
You may be kept from rising.
But no one can keep you
from lifting your heart
toward heaven—
only you.
It is in the midst of misery
that so much becomes clear.
The one who says nothing good
came of this,
is not yet listening.
—Clarissa Pinkola Estes

There Are Many Kinds of Riches | 23

I thank fate for having made me born poor.
Poverty taught me the true value of the gift useful to life.
—Anatole France

The Harvest's Yield | 24

Wheresoe'er I turn mine eyes
Around on earth or tour of the skies,
I see Thee in the story field,
I see Thee in the harvest's yield,
In every breath, and every sound,

An echo of the name is found.
The blade of grass, this simple flour,
Bear witness to Thy matchless pow'r.
My every thought, Eternal God of Heaven,
Ascends to Thee, to who all praises be given.
—**Abraham Ibn Ezra**

25 | Exultation of Larks

Birds sing after a storm; why shouldn't people feel as free
to delight in whatever sunlight remains to them?
—**Rose Fitzgerald Kennedy**

26 | Lead Me to Comfort and Peace

My life is upside down, loving God. The order of the
world is out of place, and I can't do anything to right it
again. Oh, Lord, you know the pain in my heart at all
times, and you know why: my child has died. How can it
be that my beloved child is gone? The child I cared for
with such concern in every illness, the one I held close to
my heart and promised to take care of for a lifetime, is
not here for me to care for anymore. It hurts deeply that
I wasn't able to protect this child I love with my whole
being from a death that seems so unfair. Let me feel
calm. Let me breathe deeply. Be with me in this kind of
deep and transformative pain. I now carry this darkness
with me on my back and in my heart, always. It is my
burden and my companion.

Lord, there is not a single minute of my life when this loss is not etched so keenly into my brain and heart, whether it is in the middle of a busy day or in those choking moments of grief in the solitary dark of night. Let me be grateful for every minute we had together. Let me treasure those memories and find joy in them. Help me to deal with people better. They don't know what to say. They stumble and look away when they see me. They pretend nothing has happened. I know they "don't want to remind me," but they don't understand it is with me always, always. Teach me, Lord. Tell me what you want me to do with this. What am I supposed to learn from this kind of pain? What are you calling me to do? Open my battered heart and lead me to comfort and peace. Only you can give me the peace I need. Let me feel your presence in my life.
—**Author Unknown**

Strength in Stillness | 27

May the stars carry your sadness away,
May the flowers fill your heart with beauty,
May hope forever wipe away your tears,
And, above all, may silence make you strong.
—**Chief Dan George, Tsleil-Waututh Nation**

Even If | 28

Hold on to what is good,
Even if it's a handful of earth.

Hold on to what you believe,
Even if it's a tree that stands by itself.
Hold on to what you must do,
Even if it's a long way from here.
Hold on to your life,
Even if it's easier to let go.
Hold on to my hand,
Even if someday I'll be gone away from you.
—**Crowfoot, Blackfoot Warrior and Orator**

29 | Steadfast Spirit

Create in me a pure heart, O God,
and renew a steadfast spirit within me.
Do not cast me from your presence
or take your Holy Spirit from me.
Restore to me the joy of salvation
and grant me a willing spirit to sustain me.
—**Psalm 51:10–12, King David, NIT**

30 | Speaking the Future

There will be no other words in the world
But those our children speak.
What will she make of a world
Do you suppose, of which she is made?
—**George Oppen**

Generosity of Spirit

"You can't eat beauty, it doesn't sustain you. What is fundamentally beautiful is compassion for yourself and those around you. That kind of beauty inflames the heart and enchants the soul."
—**Lupita Nyong'o**

"Gratitude is heaven itself."
—**William Blake**

"One looks back with appreciation to the brilliant teachers, but with gratitude to those who touched our human feelings."
—**Confucius**

"Forget injuries, never forget kindness."
—**Confucius**

"Gratitude is a divine emotion. It fills the heart, not to bursting; it warms it, but not to fever. I like to taste leisurely of bliss. Devoured in haste, I do not know its flavor."
—**Charlotte Bronte**

"They do not love that do not show their love."
—**William Shakespeare**

1 | Twice as Beautiful

Always remember you are braver
than you believe,
stronger than you seem,
smarter than you think,
and twice as beautiful as
you've ever imagined.
—**Dr. Seuss**

2 | Strength, Hope, Courage, and Love

Disturb us, Lord, when
We are too well pleased with ourselves,
When our dreams have come true
Because we have dreamed too little,
When we arrived safely
Because we sailed too close to the shore.

Disturb us, Lord, when
With the abundance of things we possess
We have lost our thirst
For the waters of life;
Having fallen in love with life,
We have ceased to dream of eternity
And in our efforts to build a new earth,
We have allowed our vision
Of the new Heaven to dim.

Disturb us, Lord, to dare more boldly,
To venture on wider seas

Where storms will show your mastery;
Where losing sight of land,
We shall find the stars.
We ask You to push back
The horizons of our hopes;
And to push into the future
In strength, courage, hope, and love.

Amen.
—**Daily Prayer**

Won't You Celebrate with Me | 3

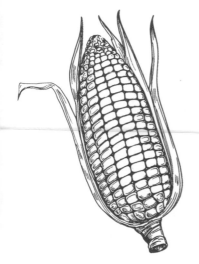

won't you celebrate with me
what i have shaped into
a kind of life? i had no model.
born in babylon
both nonwhite and woman
what did i see to be except myself?
i made it up
here on this bridge between
starshine and clay,
my one hand holding tight
my other hand; come celebrate
with me that everyday
something has tried to kill me
and has failed.
—**Lucille Clifton**

4 | In Everything Is Its Opposite

When starting out, don't worry about not having enough
money. Limited funds are a blessing, not a curse. Nothing
encourages creative thinking in quite the same way.
—H. Jackson Brown

5 | May All Your Prayers Be Answered

May God give you...
For every storm, a rainbow
For every tear, a smile
For every case, a promise
And a blessing
In each trial
For every problem life sends,
A faithful friend to share
For every sigh a sweet song
And an answer
For each prayer.
—Irish prayer

6 | Engage

Respond; don't react.
Listen; don't talk.
Think; don't assume.
—Raji Lukkoor

You Already Have Everything You Need | 7

I cannot lose anything in this place of
abundance I found.
—**St. Catherine of Siena**

May Peace Ride In | 8

Blessed be the Earth and those who tend her,
for she is the source and sustenance of our lives.

Blessed be the children who hunger for food,
learning, and homes that are safe,
for their future is shaped by our choices today.

Blessed be the refugees fleeing the violence of war
and poverty
may they find shelter, peace, and work that
sustains them.

Blessed be those who are calling for freedom,
resisting oppression and risking their lives in the
struggle for
justice,
for they are the shapers of a brighter world.

Blessed be the persecuted and wrongly judged,
for theirs is a sorrow lessened only by mercy and
human kindness.

Blessed be the prophets who speak and write of a
world beyond
war,
for theirs are the words becoming flesh.

Blessed be the storytellers, music-makers, and
artists of life,
for they are the true light of the world.

Blessed be the tender-hearted who mourn and grieve
the wars we've fought, the lives we've lost,
may peace ride in on the river of their tears.
—**Louise Harmon**

9 | Love in Action

May we love ever more.
May we motivate ourselves to committed love in action.
May we motivate ourselves to live the life
we wish to see in the
world.
May we be the transformation we wish to see in
the world.
From the inside out...
From the roots branching upwards...
From the heart
to thought
to word
to action.
Through life's trials and hardships

we can arise beautiful and free.
—"For Luna," Julia "Butterfly" Hill

Hope Is Always There | 10

Believe more deeply. Hold your face up to the light,
even though for the moment you do not see.
—Bill Wilson

Victory Over Difficulty | 11

God, I offer myself to Thee—
to build with me
and to do with me as Thou wilt.
Relieve me of the bondage of self
that I may better do Thy will.
Take away my difficulties
that victory over them may bear witness
to those I would help of Thy Power,
Thy Love, and Thy Way of life.
May I do Thy will always!
—Alcoholics Anonymous' Big Book

12 | I Am the Soft Stars That Shine at Night

Do not stand at my grave and weep
I am not there; I do not sleep.
I am a thousand winds that blow,

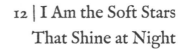

I am the diamond glints on snow,
I am the sun on ripened grain,
I am the gentle autumn rain.
When you awaken in the morning's hush,
I am the swift uplifting rush
Of quiet birds in circled flight.
I am the soft stars that shine at night.
Do not stand at my grave and cry,
I am not there; I did not die.
—Mary Elizabeth Fry

13 | Protect All Children of the Earth

Creator, open our hearts
to peace and healing between all people.

Creator, open our hearts
to provide and protect for all children of the earth.

Creator, open our hearts
to respect for the earth, and all the gifts of the earth.

Creator, open our hearts
to end exclusion, violence, and fear among all.

Thank you for the gifts of this day and every day.
—Native American Chant

Be at Peace with Yourself | 14

Everything is a miracle. It is a miracle that one does not
dissolve in one's bath like a lump of sugar.
—**Joseph Gordon-Levitt**

Lovely Are You | 15

Gratitude creates the most wonderful feeling. It can
resolve disputes. It can strengthen friendships. And it
makes us better men and women.
—**Gordon B. Hinckley**

Choices | 16

There are only two ways to live your life.
One is as though nothing is a miracle.
The other is as though everything is a miracle.
—**Albert Einstein**

Roads Not Taken | 17

I do not ask to walk smooth paths
nor bear an easy load.
I pray for strength and fortitude
to climb the rock-strewn road.

Give me such courage and I can scale
the heaviest peaks alone,

and transform every stumbling block
into a steppingstone.
—**Gail Brook Burket**

18 | Feast in Paradise

Be present at our table, Lord. Be here and everywhere
adored. Thy creatures bless and grant that we may feast
in paradise with Thee.
—**John Cennick**

19 | Crystal Clarity

What I really want to say is that, astonishingly, the
reward for truth, after all this way, is not justice or
knowledge or expertise-though these things may happen-
but joy, and the reward of kindness is not goodness or
been taught well of or even having kindness return-
though these things may happen too. No, the reward for
kindness, as well, is joy.
—**Mark Nepo**

Songs of Gratitude | 20

I always say that writing, for me, is like going to church.
When I'm out of my own way, when my ego is hushed,
when my propensity for judging myself and editing
myself is silenced for a moment, I'm feeling pretty close
to God and everything's good. To find a lyric that comes
together to teach me about myself is a real blessing.
I wrote a lot of my last record (Detours) at six in the
morning, right after feeding my baby, really enjoying
the quiet and appreciating the thoughts that come at
that hour.
—Sheryl Crow

Face Everything with Courage | 21

Dear Lord,
Thank you for the woman reading this prayer right now.
Thank you for her heart. May you bless her right now.
Fill her with your incredible peace. Wrap her in your
love. May she feel confident and worthy. I pray that she
will grow closer to you every day. Fuel a desire deep
within her to seek after you. I pray that she would lead
a life by the example Christ set. May she face everything
with courage, and may she walk in integrity. Help her
with anything she is struggling with, surround her with
encouragement, and give her your precious wisdom. May
she experience joy today in Jesus' name, Amen!
—Jennifer Smith

22 | In the Depths of My Heart

I believe there is Someone waiting for me, waiting to say:
"Welcome Home!"
Someone I have never seen, but whom I will
recognize in the depths of my heart
because He has lived there since the beginning of time.
Someone who has never doubted my return,
never failed to still my doubts about my return.
I believe there is Someone who knows me so intimately,
loves me so totally, that joy will spark spontaneously
when we reunite in the land of immortal Birth.
Tears will be wiped away;
Sadness and fear will disappear as mist when it meets the
morning sun.
This is whom I seek, seeks me.
He has never left me alone.
For He is Self of myself,
Soul of my soul,
Life of my very life.
—Sister Joan Metzner

23 | What Matters More

My shortest days end,
My lengthening days begin.
What matters more or less sun in the sky,
When all is sun within?
—Christina G. Rossetti

For the Light of Life | 24

Ground of all being,
Source of all life, Father of the universe,
Your name is sacred, beyond speaking.

May we know your presence,
may your longings be our longings in heart and in action.
May there be food for the human family today
and for the whole earth community.

Forgive us the falseness of what we have done
as we forgive those who are untrue to us.

Do not forsake us in our time of conflict
but lead us into new beginnings.

For the light of life, the vitality of life,
and the glory of life are yours, now and forever.

Amen.
—**The Casa Del Sol Prayer of Jesus**

All You Own Is Yourself | 25

Let it go, let it leave, let it happen. Nothing in this world
was promised or belonged to you anyway.
—**Rupi Kaur**

26 | Reverence for All Life

From childhood, I felt a compassion for animals.
Even before I started school, I found it impossible
to understand why, in my evening prayers,
I should pray only for human beings.
Consequently, after my mother had prayed with me
and had given me a goodnight kiss, I secretly
recited another prayer, one I had composed myself.
It went like this:

Dear God, protect and bless all living beings.
Keep them from evil and let them sleep in peace.
—**Dr. Albert Schweitzer**

27 | Prayer to Start Every Day

Don't worry,
be happy!
—**Meher Baba**

28 | The Good Road and the Road of Difficulties

Hey-a-a-hey! Hey-a-a-hey! Hey-a-a-hey! Hey-a-a-hey!

Grandfather, Great Spirit, once more behold
me on earth
and lean to hear my feeble voice.

You lived first, and you are older than all need,
older than all
prayer.
All things belong to you—the two-leggeds,
the four-leggeds, the wings of the air
and all green things that live.
You have set the powers of the four quarters
to cross each other.
The good road and road of difficulties
you have made to cross;
and where they cross, the place is holy.
Day in and day out, forever, you are the life of things.

Therefore I am sending a voice, Great Spirit,
my Grandfather, forgetting nothing you have made,
the stars of the universe
and the grasses of the earth.

You have said to me,
when I was still young and could hope,
that in difficulty I should send a voice four times,
once for each quarter of the earth,
and you would hear me.

To-day I send a voice for a people in despair.

You have given me a sacred pipe,
and through this I should make my offering.
You see it now.

From the west, you have given me the cup
of living water and the sacred bow,

the power to make life and to destroy.
You have given me a sacred wind and the herb
from where the white giant lives—
the cleansing power and the healing.
The daybreak star and the pipe,
you have given from the east;
and from the south, the nation's sacred hoop
and the tree that was to bloom.
To the center of the world you have taken me
and showed the goodness and the beauty
and the strangeness of the greening earth, the
only mother—
and there the spirit shapes of things,
as they should be,
you have shown to me and I have seen.
At the center of this sacred hoop you have said
that I should make the tree to bloom.

With tears running, O Great Spirit, Great Spirit,
my Grandfather

—

with running tears I must say now that
the tree has never bloomed.
A pitiful old man, you see me here,
and I have fallen away and have done nothing.
Here at the center of the world,
where you took me when I was young and taught me;
here, old, I stand, and the tree is withered,
Grandfather, my Grandfather!

Again, and maybe the last time on this earth,
I recall the great vision you sent me.

It may be that some little root of the sacred tree
still lives.
Nourish it then, that it may leaf and bloom
and fill with singing birds.
Hear me, not for myself, but for my people; I am old.
Hear me that they may once more go back into the
sacred hoop
and find the good red road, the shielding tree!

In sorrow I am sending a feeble voice,
O Six Powers of the World.
Hear me in my sorrow, for I may never call again.
O make my people live!
—**Black Elk**

Angels Round My Head | 29

Matthew, Mark, Luke and John,
The bed be blest that I lie on.
Four corners to my bed,
Four angels round my head;
One to watch, and one to pray,
And two to bear my soul away.
—**Seventeenth century child's bedtime prayer**

Enough Is a Gift | 30

Be thankful for what you have; you'll end up
having more. If you concentrate on what you don't

have, you will never, ever have enough.
—**Oprah Winfrey**

31 | How to Not Block the Blessings

There's a reason the sun rises anew each day.
Every day is a completely clean slate.
Cherry-picking bad memories
and rolling them around in my head all day,
it's hard to remember that
I've been blessed with forgiveness.
Forever. For good.
—**Ruth Williams**

Everyday Kindness

"When eating bamboo sprouts, remember the man who
planted them."
—**Chinese Proverb**

"Gratitude bestows reverence, allowing us to encounter
everyday epiphanies, those transcendent moments of
awe that change forever how we experience life and
the world."
—**John Milton**

"When you arise in the morning, think of what a
precious privilege it is to be alive—to breathe, to think,
to enjoy, to love."
—**Marcus Aurelius**

"The roots of all goodness lie in the soil of appreciation
for goodness."
—**The Dalai Lama**

"Appreciation is a wonderful thing. It makes what is
excellent in others belong to us as well."
—**Voltaire**

"When I'm not thank'd at all, I'm thank'd enough, I've
done my duty, and I've done no more."
—**Henry Fielding**

1 | Truth, Life, and Love

Father-Mother God,
Loving me—
Guard me when I sleep;
Guide my little feet
Up to Thee.
—**Mary Baker Eddy**

2 | Living on Track

When we are on track, living close to the things we deem
important—the things we value—we feel happier. This
isn't flash happiness, it isn't the kind that lasts for a few
minutes when we get a new toy or enjoy a concert. This
is the kind that lingers in the background of our lives.
The kind that even in moments of sadness or frustration,
never completely disappears, because if we are living
in a values-based life we are also living with meaning
and purpose.
—**Polly Campbell**

3 | Be Filled with Deep and Abiding Peace

Deep peace I breathe into you, O weariness, here:
O ache, here!
Deep peace, a soft white dove to You;
Deep peace, a quiet rain to you;
Deep peace, an ebbing wave to you!
Deep peace, red wind of the east from you;

Deep peace, grey wind of the west to You;
Deep peace, dark wind of the north from you;
Deep peace, blue wind of the south to you!
Deep peace, pure red of the flame to you;
Deep peace, pure white of the moon to you;
Deep peace, pure green of the grass to you;
Deep peace, pure brown of the earth to you;
Deep peace, pure grey of the dew to you,
Deep peace, pure blue of the sky to you!
Deep peace of the running wave to you,
Deep peace of the flowing air to you...
—Fiona Macleod

Love Is All Around | 4

Love is easy. You can't resist love. You get an idea, someone says something, and you're in love. I went to dinner in Denver about twenty years ago and heard the lady at the next table say to her friend, "Oh my God, I'll bet dogs think every day is Christmas." I went up to her and said, "Ma'am, thank you. You've just given me a title. I'm going back to my hotel, and I'm going to write a book called Dogs Think That Every Day Is Christmas." That's how these things happen.
—Ray Bradbury

5 | You Have All You Need

Gratitude unlocks the fullness of life. It turns what
we have into enough, and more. It turns denial into
acceptance, chaos to order, confusion to clarity. It can
turn a meal into a feast, a house into a home, a stranger
into a friend. Gratitude makes sense of our past, brings
peace for today and creates a vision for tomorrow.
—**Melody Beattie**

6 | Slowing Down to Savor Life

Let us not get so busy or live so fast that we can't listen
to the music of the meadow or the symphony that
glorifies the forest. Some things in the world are far
more important than wealth; one of them is the ability
to enjoy simple things.
—**Dale Carnegie**

7 | We All Come from Source

All dreams spin out from the same web.
—**Hopi Tribe**

I think happiness is what makes you pretty. Period.
Happy people are beautiful. They become like a mirror
and they reflect that happiness.
—**Drew Barrymore**

Song of Spirit | 9

I am the wind on the sea
I am the ocean wave
I am the sound of the billows.
I am the seven-horned stag
I am the hawk on the cliff
I am the dewdrop in sunlight
I am the fairest of flowers
I am the raging boar
I am the salmon in the deep pool
I am the lake on the plain
I am the meaning of the poem
I am the point of the spear
I am the god who makes fire in the head
Who levels the mountain?
Who speaks the age of the moon?
Who has been where the sun sleeps?
Who, if not I?
—**Ancient Celtic Invocation; The Song of Amergin**

10 | Do the Very Best You Can

Friends do it this way—that is,
whatever you do in life,
do the very best you can
with both your heart and mind.

And if you do it that way,
the Power of the Universe
will come to your assistance,
if your heart and mind are in Unity.

When one sits in the Hoop of The People,
one must be responsible because
All of Creation is related.
And the Hurt of one is the hurt of all.
And the honor of one is the honor of all.
And whatever we do affects everything in the universe.

If you do it that way—that is,
if you truly join your heart and mind
as One-whatever you ask for,
that is the Way it's Going to be.
**—Lakota Instructions for Living passed down from
White Buffalo Calf Woman**

11 | Be Lifted from Your Sorrows

As you leave this place
may the Living Lord go with you;
May he go behind you, to encourage you,

beside you, to befriend you,
above you, to watch over you,
beneath you, to lift you from your sorrows,
within you, to give you the gifts of faith, hope, and love,
and always before you, to show you the way.
—**Benediction**

The Key to a Happy Life | 12

Gratefulness is the key to a happy life that we hold in
our hands, because if we are not grateful, then no matter
how much we have we will not be happy, because we will
always want to have something else or something more.
—**Brother David Steindl-Rast**

Pausing to Appreciate | 13

Whatever our individual troubles and challenges may be,
it's important to pause every now and then to appreciate
all that we have, on every level. We need to literally
"count our blessings," give thanks for them, allow
ourselves to enjoy them, and relish the experience of
prosperity we already have.
—**Shakti Gawain**

Second Chances | 14

We give thanks for all those times we have arisen from
the depths or simply taking a tiny step toward something

new. May we be empowered by extraordinary second chances. And as we enter the world anew, let us turn the tides of despair into endless waves of hope.
—**Molly Fumia**

15 | Remember to Give Thanks

All this is God,
right here in my pea-green house
each morning
and I mean,
though often forget,
to give thanks...
—**Anne Sexton**

16 | Glimpses of the Divine

Goodness is all around us
But verily, most of it
I have yet to let in
Yet to discover

After a life of mainly ego
Catching only glimpses
Of the divine traits
I want to change

I want the glimpses,
Those fantastic glimpses
No longer be glimpses

But become the main

Cumulonimbi of peace
Palaces of silence
Love and love and love
Generosity beyond control

O my God turn my every minute
into one of those glimpses
—**Chapel of the Woods**

Good Days | 17

What good is the warmth of summer,
without the cold winter to give it sweetness.
—**John Steinbeck**

Bright as Day | 18

Last night when I walked the dog here in Wisconsin,
it was minus 15 degrees—minus 26 with the wind
chill, according to the weather site... Having said that,
even walking last night in minus 26, the air was so
preternaturally clear, the moon was actually doing
that "shining bright as day" thing, the shadows just fell
perfectly to the snow, and the stars looked like they'd
been draped by a Hollywood set designer. The beauty,
even as my skin-where it was exposed to the cold air-

actually hurt, was still so overwhelming and so peaceful.
That's a blessing.
—Neil Gaiman

19 | Taste & See

Full of splendor and beauty
Full of life.
Of souls hidden Souls Hidden,
Of treasures of the Holy Spirit,
Of fountains of stream,
Of greatness and beauty
Profoundly I ascend
Toward the heights of the World Soul
That gives life to the universe.
How majestic the vision
Come, enjoy,
Come, find peace,
Embrace delight,
Taste and see that God is good.
Why spend your substance on what does not nourish
And your labor on why cannot satisfy?
Listen to me, and you will enjoy what is good,
And find delight in what is truly precious.
—Abraham Isaac Kook

20 | There Is a Comfort for Every Sorrow

The best remedy for those who are
afraid, lonely, or unhappy is to go outside,

somewhere where they can be quiet,
alone with the heavens, nature, and God.
Because only then does one feel that all
is as it should be,
and that God wishes to see people happy,
amidst the simple beauty of nature.
As long as this exists, and it certainly
always will, I know that then there will
always be comfort for every sorrow,
whatever the circumstances may be.
And I firmly believe that nature
brings solace in all troubles.
—**Anne Frank**

Love and Kindness Will Always Be in My Heart | 21

Father, help me to be a capable, intelligent,
and virtuous woman—faithful, diligent, generous,
and spiritually strong.
May the law of love and kindness
always be in my heart and on my lips.
In Jesus' name, Amen.
—**Alisha Gratehouse**

Praise Ye Truth | 22

O praise the Lord,
all ye nations;
praise him, all ye people.

For his merciful kindness is great toward us;
and the truth of the Lord endureth forever.
Praise ye the Lord.
—**Psalm 117:1, KJV**

23 | Your Heart Is a Beating Drum

I am the drum,
you are the drum, and we are the drum.
Rhythm is the soul of life.
The whole universe revolves in rhythm.
Everything and every human action revolve in rhythm.
—**Babatunde Olatunji**

24 | Beatitudes

Blessed be the Earth and those who tend her,
for she is the source and sustenance of our lives.

Blessed be the children who hunger for food,
learning, and homes that are safe,
for their future is shaped by our choices today.

Blessed be the refugees fleeing the violence of war
and poverty,
may they find shelter, peace, and work that
sustains them.

Blessed be those who are calling for freedom,

resisting oppression, and risking their lives in the
struggle for justice,
for they are the shapers of a brighter world.

Blessed be the persecuted and wrongly judged,
for theirs is a sorrow lessened only by mercy and
human kindness.

Blessed be the prophets who speak and write of a world
beyond war,
for theirs are the words becoming flesh.

Blessed be the storytellers, music-makers, and
artists at life,
for they are the true light of the world.

Blessed be the tender-hearted who mourn and grieve
the wars we've fought, the lives we've lost,
may peace ride in on the river of their tears.
— **Cathedral of Light**

Life Is Short: Be Kind | 25

Life is short, and we have not too much time
for gladdening the hearts of those
who are traveling the dark way with us.
Oh, be swift to love! Make haste to be kind.
—**Henri-Frederic Amiel**

26 | Asking the Blessing of the Triple Goddess

I am bowing my head
In the eye of the Mother who gave me birth,
In the eye of the Maiden who loves me,
In the eye of the Crone who guides me in wisdom,

In friendship and affection.

Through thy gift of nature, O Goddess,
Bestow upon us fullness in our need.

Love towards the Lady,
The affection of the Lady,
The laughter of the Lady,
The wisdom of the Lady,
The passion of the Lady,
The blessing of the Lady,
And the magic of the Lady

To do in the world of Abred
As the Ageless Ones do in Gwynfyd;

Each shade and light,
Each day and night,
Each moment in kindness,
Grant us Thy Sight.
—**Ancient Celtic Song**

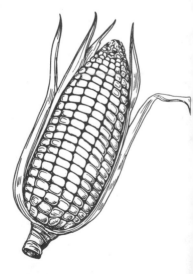

LET US GIVE THANKS

A Time for Change | 27

If you stay stuck for a period of time,
this is given unto you by your soul
to give you a resting place.
At this place, you judge it as stuck.
See it as transition.
—Kuan Yin

Just Create Love | 28

Kindness in words creates confidence,
Kindness in thinking creates profoundness,
Kindness in giving creates love.
—Lao Tzu

Forgiveness, Kindness, Tolerance | 29

Fountain of Everlasting Peace and Healing Balm,
Wash over our wounds of war, violence, and hatred,
Scrub deep the stains that destroy the fabric of
Your Existence,
Mend the tattered threads of the Cloak of Your Majesty,
The delicate web of the universe which is Your
Life and Love...
A prophet of nonviolence You have raised up for Truth,
Reflecting the Source of Your Unfathomable Wisdom,
Flowing from the One Great Abyss of Creation's Glory,
Open our minds to hear Your Voice speaking
Peace this day,

Born from One Cosmic Egg, we are one family in You,
Help us to learn forgiveness, kindness, tolerance,
Greatness of mind and heart,
So that destroying all weapons of war,
Burying all animosities and differences,
We may hear the Divine Harmony of Your Love,
Preserving our blue-jewel-earth-planet,
Spinning the dance of a Mother's Infinite Tenderness,
That draws all into Unity in one Compassionate Heart.
Bestow the Blissful Smile of sun and rain
which is Your Divine Presence
Making Peace grow in our hearts as seeds for a new era,
Birthing the song of nonviolence
Which blesses our world
with Peace Eternal.
—**Sister Rosemarie**

30 | Be with Us and Hear Us

Fire of the Spirit,
Life of the lives of creatures,
Spiral of sanctity,
Bond of all natures,
Glow of charity,
Lights of clarity,
Taste of sweetness to the fallen,
Be with us and hear us.
—**Hildegarde of Bingen**

Sparking the Flame Within

"No kind action ever stops with itself. One kind action leads to another. Good example is followed. A single act of kindness throws out roots in all directions, and the roots spring up and make new trees. The greatest work that kindness does to others is that it makes them kind themselves."
—Amelia Earhart

"Don't complain about what you don't have. Use what you've got. To be less than your best is a sin."
—Oprah Winfrey

"The world is more malleable than you think and it's waiting for you to hammer it into shape."
—Bono

"It is only normal that / People count losses with / their minds, / and ignore / to count blessings / with the graciousness / of their hearts."
—Suzy Kassem

"You have no cause for anything but gratitude and joy."
—Buddha

1 | A Child's Gratitude

Goodnight God.
I hope you are having
a good time being the world.
I like the world very much
I'm glad you made the plants
and trees survive with the
rain and summers. ·
When summer is nearly near
the leaves begin to fall.
I hope you have a good time
being the world.
I like how God feels around
everyone in the world.
God, I am very happy that
I live on you.
Your arms clasp around the world.
—**Louise Baxter**

2 | God Bless Me

Little Boy kneels at the foot of the bed,
Droops on the little hands little gold head.
Hush! Hush! Whisper who dares!
Christopher Robin is saying his prayers.

God bless Mummy. I know that's right.
Wasn't it fun in the bath tonight?
The cold's so cold, and the hot's so hot.
Oh! God Bless Daddy—I quite forgot.

If I open my fingers a little bit more,
I can see Nanny's dressing gown on the door.
It's a beautiful blue, but it hasn't a hood.
Oh! God bless Nanny and make her good.

Mine has a hood and if I lie in bed,
And put the hood right over my head,
And I shut my eyes, and I curl up small,
Nobody knows that I'm there at all.

Oh! Thank you, God, for a lovely day.
And what was the other I had to say?
I said, "Bless Daddy," so what can it be?
Oh! Now I remember. God Bless me.

Little boy kneels at the foot of the bed,
Droops on the little hands little gold head,
Hush! Hush! Whisper who dares!
Christopher Robin is saying his prayers.
—**A. A. Milne**

Strength in Trouble | 3

As the rain hides the stars,
as the autumn mist
hides the hills,
as the clouds veil
the blue of the sky, so
the dark happenings of my lot
hide the shining of thy face from me.

Yet, if I may hold thy hand in the darkness,
it is enough, since I know
that though I may stumble in my going,
Thou dost not fall.
—Scottish Song

4 | The Irresistible Rhythm of Life

Are you lookin' for me?
are you?
are you lookin' for ME?
well you won't find me
'cause I'll be DANCIN'!
I'll be dancin' with the THUNDER
and the IRRESISTIBLE RHYTHM of LIFE!
—Orunamamu, Storyteller

5 | Be a Student of Life

May your journey
through the universal questions of life
bring you to a new moment of awareness.
May it be an enlightening one.

May you find embedded in the past,
like all the students of life before you,
the answers you are seeking now.

May they awaken that in you which is
deeper than fact,

truer than fiction,
full of faith.

May you come to know
that in every human event
is a particle of the Divine
to which we turn for meaning here,
to which we tend for fullness of life hereafter.
—**Sister Joan Chittister**

A List of Love | 6

Stop for a moment and be thankful for the giver behind
the gift. Make a list of the people in your life who made
you happy today.
—**Brenda Knight**

Four Very Important Sentences in Life | 7

Please forgive me.
I forgive you.
Thank you.
I love you.
—**Dr. Ira Byock**

Teach Me to Serve as I Should | 8

Dearest Lord, teach me to be generous,
teach me to serve you as I should,

to give and not to count the cost,
to fight and not to heed the wounds,
to toil and not to seek for rest,
to labor and ask not for reward,
save that of knowing that I do your most holy will.
—St. Ignatius Loyola

9 | Poetry Is Prayer

poetry is prayer
light dancing inside words
five times a day
I try to write
step by step
I move towards the mihrab
I prepare to recite
what is in my heart
I recite your name.
—E. Ethelbert Miller

10 | Do Not Despair

Let no sadness come to this heart.
Let not trouble come to these arms.
Let no conflict come to these eyes.
Let my soul be filled
with the blessing of joy and peace.
—Hamsa Prayer

Strength for the Journey | 11

My True Father,
I set my hopes upon You alone,
And I only ask You, God,
For my Soul salvation.
Let Your Holy Will
Be my strengthening on this way,
For my life without You is a mere empty moment,
And only serving You leads to Eternal life.
Amen!
—**St. Agapit of Pechersk**

In Dangerous Weather | 12

God, ransack the little ordered
rooms of my dignity, and cast
me out into wide and dangerous
weathers of my deepest needs.
—**Author Unknown**

Just Don't Forget to Keep It Open | 13

The universe will bring people whatever they want...
Let the magic happen. It's always there.
Abundance and love are always there.
Believe in the highest good.
There is a higher essence to everything.
The realm you're in has a heaviness that mutes energy.

You can penetrate through it, no matter how dark
and heavy.
Sometimes it has nothing to do with karma.
Just don't forget to keep it open.
Don't get too bogged down...
Prosperity can happen at any time.
I want to give you everything that you need.
—**Kuan Yin**

14 | Deliver Me

Dear God,
Deliver me to my passion.
Deliver me to my brilliance.
Deliver me to my intelligence.
Deliver me to my depth.
Deliver me to my nobility.
Deliver me to my beauty.
Deliver me to my power to heal.
Deliver me to You.
—**Marianne Williamson**

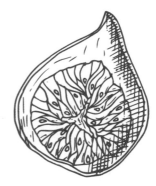

15 | Bring Peace and Comfort to Us

Heavenly Father

I call on you. I ask you to touch [us] with your
healing power.
Cast out all sickness and recreate [us].
Let the warmth of your healing love pass through [us].

Lord grant that [we] will be free from pain,
from anxiety, and from discomfort.
Please allow your love and the compassion of caregivers,
family and friends to bring peace and comfort to [us].
This we ask through Christ, our Lord.
Amen.
—Walter Whitmore

The Little Things in Life | 16

Give thanks for a little and you will find a lot.
—Hausa Proverb

Find Your Gifts and Use Them | 17

The greatest tragedy in life is not death;
the greatest tragedy takes place
when our talents and capabilities are underutilized
and allowed to rust while we are living.
—Amma

One We Are | 18

We light the light of a new idea.
It is the light of our coming together.
It is the light of our growing;
to know new things,
to see new beauty,

to feel new love.
—**Unitarian Chalice Lighting Invocation**

19 | What Is Your Service to the World?

God,
I'm willing
to do your work.
Please
show me what it is.
—**Tami Simon**

20 | It's Ok to Be Vulnerable

Don't worry, it's going to be OK.
It's all right, little one, you're safe and loved.
It's OK to cry, it's OK to be afraid, it's OK to be weak,
it's OK to be vulnerable, it's OK to be human.
It's from all these elements that we grow,
and it's from all these elements that I am born
out of you.
I Love You.
—**Author Unknown**

21 | All Things Calm

You are the peace of all things calm
You are the place to hide from harm
You are the light that shines in the dark

You are the heart's eternal spark
You are the door that's open wide
You are the guest who waits inside
You are the stranger at the door
You are the calling of the poor
You are my Lord and save me from ill
You are the light, the truth, the way
You are my Savior this very day.
—**Medieval Celtic Chant**

Grant Me a Perfect End | 22

Gracious and Holy Father,
Please give me:
intellect to understand you,
reason to discern you,
diligence to seek you,
wisdom to find you,
a spirit to know you,
a heart to meditate upon you,
ears to hear you,
eyes to see you,
a tongue to proclaim you,
a way of life pleasing to you,
patience to wait for you
and perseverance to look for you.
Grant me a perfect end,
your holy presence,
a blessed resurrection
and life everlasting.

Amen.
—St. Benedict of Nursiaca

23 | Know There Is Love in the World

At the center of the universe is a
loving heart that continues to beat
and that wants the best for every person.
Anything we can do to help foster
the intellect and spirit and emotional growth
of our fellow human beings, that is our job.
Those of us who have this particular vision
must continue against all odds.
Life is for service.
—Fred Rogers, MISTER ROGERS'S NEIGHBORHOOD

24 | Endless Radiance

O love, O pure deep love, be here, be now—be all;
Worlds dissolve into your stainless endless radiance,
Frail living leaves burn with you brighter than cold stars.
Make me your servant, your breath, your core.
—Sufi Song

25 | Let Me Be a Living Example of Love

Dear Jesus, I confess to you my failures to love.
I thank and praise you for your work of paying
for all those failures and loving perfectly in my place.

I trust your promise that the Father will give
me anything
I ask in your name. I now pray for greater and greater
Christ-like love in all my relationships. Work in me
to bear more and more fruit, to your glory.
In your saving name, I confidently pray. Amen.
—**Mollie Schairer**

Keep Dreaming | 26

If you can dream it, you can do it.
—**Walt Disney**

The Warmth of Our Nearness | 27

God, you are like a mother to us all,
nourishing all creatures with food and with blessing.
Strengthen my child with (my milk, this food)
and with the warmth of our nearness.
—**Nurses of Faith**

Quiet the Mind | 28

God, please put a guard at my mouth,
love in my heart
and calm in my mind.
Amen.
—**Julie Lepianka**

29 | Live the Questions Now

Have patience with everything unresolved in your heart
and try to love the questions themselves...
Don't search for the answers,
which could not be given to you now,
because you would not be able to live with them.
And the point is to live everything.
Live the questions now.
Perhaps then, someday far in the future,
you will gradually, without even noticing it,
live your way into the answer.
—Rainer Maria Rilke

30 | Through the Peace of the Evening

I speak to you.
Be still
Know I am God.

I spoke to you when you were born.
Be still
Know I am God.

I spoke to you at your first sight.
Be still
Know I am God.

I spoke to you at your first word.
Be still
Know I am God.

I spoke to you at your first thought.
Be still
Know I am God.

I spoke to you at your first love.
Be still
Know I am God.

I spoke to you at your first song.
Be still
Know I am God...
—**Essene Gospel of Peace**

Walk the Good Road to the Day of Quiet | 31

There is no other one to pray to but you.
You yourself, everything that you see,
everything that has been made by you.
The star nations all over the universe you have finished.
The four quarters of the earth you have finished.
The day, and in that day, everything you have finished.
Grandfather, Great Spirit, lean close to the earth
that you may hear the voice I send.
You towards where the sun goes down, behold me;
Thunder Beings, behold me!
You where the White Giant lives in power, behold me!
You where the sun shines continually,
whence come the daybreak star and the day, behold me!
You where the summer lives, behold me!

You in the depths of the heavens, an eagle of
power, behold!
And you, Mother Earth, the only Mother,
you who have shown mercy to your children.

Hear me, four quarters of the world—a relative I am!
Give me the strength to walk the soft earth, a relative to
all that is!
Give me the eyes to see and the strength to understand,
that I may be like you.
With your power only can I face the winds
and walk the good road to the day of quiet.

This is my prayer; hear me!
The voice I have sent is weak,
yet with earnestness I have sent it.
Hear me!

It is finished. Hetchetu aloh!
—**Oglala Sioux**

Bounty of Blessings

"Gratitude therefore takes nothing for granted, is never unresponsive, is constantly awakening to new wonder, and to praise of the goodness of God. For the grateful person knows that God is good, not by hearsay but by experience. And that is what makes all the difference."
—**Thomas Merton**

"I never regret anything. Because every little detail of your life is what made you into who you are in the end."
—**Drew Barrymore**

"Do not let the empty cup be your first teacher of the blessings you had when it was full."
—**Alexander Maclaren**

"Gratitude is a vaccine, an antitoxin and an antiseptic."
—**John henry Jowett**

"Let us rise up and be thankful, for if we didn't learn a lot today, at least we learned a little."
—**Buddha**

"If you count all your assets, you always show a profit."
—**Robert Quillen**

1 | Rise in Gratitude

Keep a pen and a journal next to your bed, and before you rise every morning, make a list of all that you're grateful for, realizing that gratitude will magnetize good things and good people to you. Gratitude also helps us open our hearts for the day.
—**Rhonda Byrne**

2 | For Those Who Need Employment

Heavenly Father, we remember before you
those who suffer want and anxiety from lack of work.
Guide the people of this land to use
our public and private wealth
so that all may find suitable and fulfilling employment
and receive just payment for their labor;
through Jesus Christ our Lord. Amen...
—**Morning Star Church**

3 | Catch the Trade Winds in Your Sails

Twenty years from now
you will be more disappointed by the things that you
didn't do than by the ones you did do.
So, throw off the bowlines.
Sail away from the safe harbor. Catch the trade winds in
your sails. Explore. Dream. Discover.
—**H. Jackson Brown Jr.**

Renew, release, let go. Yesterday's gone.
There's nothing you can do to bring it back. You can't
"should've" done something. You can only do something
Renew yourself.
Release that attachment.
Today is a new day!
—**Steve Maraboli**

The Spirit Will Be Alive Among Us | 5

Show me the suffering of the most miserable;
So I will know my people's plight.

Free me to pray for others;
For you are present in every person.

Help me take responsibility for my own life;
So that I can be free at last.

Grant me courage to serve others;
For in service there is true life.

Give me honesty and patience;
So that the Spirit will be alive among us.

Let the Spirit flourish and grow;
So that we will never tire of the struggle.

Let us remember those who have died for justice;

For they have given us life.

Help us love even those who hate us;
So we can change the world.

Amen.
—César E. Chávez

6 | Be Kind Anyway

People are often unreasonable, illogical and self-centered;
Forgive them anyway.

If you are kind, people may accuse you of selfish,
ulterior motives;
Be kind anyway.

If you are successful, you will win some false friends and
some true enemies;
Succeed anyway.

If you are honest and frank, people may cheat you;
Be honest and frank anyway.

What you spend years building, someone could
destroy overnight;
Build anyway.

If you find serenity and happiness, they may be jealous;
Be happy anyway.

The good you do today, people will often
forget tomorrow;
Do good anyway.

Give the world the best you have, and it may never
be enough;
Give the world the best you've got anyway.

You see, in the final analysis, it is between you
and your God;
It was never between you and them anyway.
—**Mother Teresa**

Giving Shade | 7

Gratitude is looking on the brighter side of life,
even if it means hurting your eyes.
—**Ellen DeGeneres**

Stay Grateful | 8

A thankful person is thankful under all circumstances.
A complaining soul complains even if he lives
in paradise.
— **Bahá'u'lláh**

With a Pure Heart | 9

Carry out a random act of kindness,

with no expectation of reward,
safe in the knowledge
that one day someone
might do the same for you.
—**Princess Diana**

10 | Heavenly Father Feeds Them

Look at the birds of the air;
they do not sow or reap or store away in barns,
and yet your heavenly Father feeds them.
Are you not much more valuable than they?
Can any one of you by worrying add a single hour to
your life?
—**Matthew 6:26–27**

11 | Royal Wisdom

Any charitable act is love in motion,
and love needs no publicity because love just is.
—**Prince**

12 | May Peace Ride In

Blessed be the storytellers, music-makers, and
artists at life,
for they are the true light of the world.

Blessed be the tender-hearted who mourn and grieve

the wars we've fought, the lives we've lost,
may peace ride in on the river of their tears.
—Jan Phillips

Just Savor Today | 13

Tethered to our smartphones, we are too caught up and
distracted to take the time necessary to sort through
complexity or to locate submerged purpose. In
our urgent
rush to get "there," we are going everywhere but being
nowhere. Far too busy managing with
transactive speed, we
rarely step back to lead with transformative significance.
—**Kevin Cashman**

Let the Mountains Teach Our Hearts | 14

Let the rain come and wash away
the ancient grudges, the bitter hatreds
held and nurtured over generations.
Let the rain wash away the memory
of the hurt, the neglect.
Then let the sun come out and
fill the sky with rainbows.
Let the warmth of the sun heal us
wherever we are broken.
Let it burn away the fog so that
we can see each other clearly.
So that we can see beyond labels,

beyond accents, gender or skin color.
Let the warmth and brightness
of the sun melt our selfishness.
So that we can share the joys and
feel the sorrows of our neighbors.
And let the light of the sun
be so strong that we will see all
people as our neighbors.
Let the earth, nourished by rain,
bring forth flowers
to surround us with beauty.
And let the mountains teach our hearts
to reach upward to heaven.
Amen.
—**Rabbi Harold Kushner**

15 | Be Calm, Always

Peace.
It does not mean to be in a place
where there is no noise,
trouble, or hard work.
It means to be in the midst
of those things and still be calm in your heart.
—**Author Unknown**

I Plant with All the Heart in Mind | 16

Feelings, whether of compassion or irritation,
should be welcomed, recognized, and treated
on an absolutely equal basis;
because both are ourselves.
The tangerine I am eating is me.
The mustard greens I am planting are me.
I plant with all my heart and mind.
I clean this teapot with the kind of attention
I would have were I giving
the baby Buddha or Jesus a bath.
Nothing should be treated more carefully
than anything else.
—Thich Nhất Hạnh

Don't Hurry, Don't Worry | 17

Never be in a hurry,
do everything quietly
and in a calm spirit.
Do not lose your inner peace
for anything whatsoever,
even if your whole world seems upset.
—St. Francis de Sales

Rise Upward | 18

The ceremony of lifting up our hands in prayer

is designed to remind us that we are far
removed from God,
unless our thoughts rise upward.
—John Calvin

19 | What Is My Purpose?

Help me to find my happiness
in my acceptance of what is my purpose
in friendly eyes, in work well done,
in quietness born of trust.
And most of all
in the awareness of spirit in my being.
—Hebridean Celtic Blessing

20 | Learn & Teach

When you learn, teach; when you get, give.
—Maya Angelou

21 | Diamonds and Pearls

Every day I feel is a blessing from God. And I consider it
a new beginning. Yeah, everything is beautiful.
—Prince

Prayer to Heal the Body | 22

Beloved Lord, Almighty God,
Through the Rays of the Sun,
Through the Waves of the Air,
Through the All-Pervading Life in Space;
Purify and Revivify Us
And we pray, heal our bodies, hearts, and souls.
Amen
—Piro-Murshid Hazrat Inayat Khan

Stand in Your Own Power | 23

I stand in my own power now, the questions of
permission that I used to choke on for my every meal
now dead in a fallen heap, and when they tell me that I
will fall, I nod. I will fall, I reply, and

my words are a whisper
my words are a howl

I will fall, I say, and the tumbling will be all my own.
The skinned palms and oozing knees are holy wounds,
stigmata of my She.

I will catch my own spilled blood,
and not a drop will be wasted.
—Beth Morey

24 | One Moment at a Time

Living one day at a time,
Enjoying one moment at a time,
Accepting hardship as a pathway to peace,
Taking, as Jesus did,
This sinful world as it is,
Not as I would have it,
Trusting that You will make all things right,
If I surrender to Your will,
So that I may be reasonably happy in this life,
And supremely happy with You forever in the next.
Amen.
—Reinhold Niebuhr

25 | Put Down Your Burdens

Humble yourselves,
therefore, under God's mighty hand,
that he may lift you up in due time.
Cast all your anxiety on him
because he cares for you.
—1 Peter 5:6–7

26 | Each Bright Galaxy

Time says "Let there be"
every moment and instantly
there is space and the radiance
of each bright galaxy.

And eyes beholding radiance.
And the gnats' flickering dance.
And the seas' expanse.
And death, and chance.

Time makes room
for going and coming home
and in time's womb
begins all ending.

Time is being and being
time, it is all one thing,
the shining, the seeing,
the dark abounding.
—**Ursula K. Le Guin**

The Key to Wisdom | 27

The best and safest thing
is to keep a balance in your life,
acknowledge the great powers around us and in us.
If you can do that, and live that way,
you are really a wise man.
—**Euripides**

We Are All One | 28

We light the light of a new idea.
It is the light of our coming together.

It is the light of our growing;
to know new things,
to see new beauty,
to feel new love.
—**Unitarian Invocation**

29 | Do Not Hesitate

I've made tons of mistakes over the past years,
but if there's anything I've done well,
if I see an opportunity,
or if I see God moving
or going in a direction
or opening a door for me,
I try to take it;
I try not to hesitate.
—**Shaun King**

30 | Have Hope

For what it's worth...it's never too late, or in my case
too early, to be whoever you want to be. There's no time
limit. Start whenever you want. You can change or stay
the same. There are no rules to this thing. We can make
the best or the worst of it. I hope you make the best of
it. I hope you see things that startle you. I hope you feel
things you've never felt before. I hope you meet people
who have a different point of view. I hope you live a life

you're proud of, and if you're not, I hope you have the
courage to start over again.
—**F. Scott Fitzgerald**

Everyday Succeed | 31

Gratitude is the intention to count your blessings every
day, every minute, while avoiding, whenever possible, the
belief that you need or deserve different circumstances.
—**Timothy Ray Miller**

SEPTEMBER

All Things Great and Good

"A grateful mind is a great mind which eventually attracts to itself great things."
—**Plato**

"Courtesies of a small and trivial character are the ones which strike deepest in the grateful and appreciating heart."
—**Henry Clay**

"A tree is known by its fruit; a man by his deeds. A good deed is never lost; he who sows courtesy reaps friendship, and he who plants kindness gathers love."
—**St. Basil of Caesarea**

"When you arise in the morning, give thanks for the morning light, for your life and strength. Give thanks for your food, and the joy of living. If you see no reason for giving thanks, the fault lies with yourself."
—**Tecumseh, Shawnee Chief**

"Gratitude is happiness doubled by wonder."
—**GK Chesterton**

"The unthankful heart discovers no mercies; but the thankful heart will find, in every hour, some heavenly blessings"
—**Henry Ward Beecher**

Grateful for the Daily Bread | 1

God is Great, God is Good;
Let us thank Him for our food.
By His hands we all are fed,
Give us, Lord, our Daily Bread.
Amen...
—**Author Unknown**

Find the Beauty in Others | 2

To laugh often and much; to win the respect of the intelligent people and the affection of children; to earn the appreciation of honest critics and endure the betrayal of false friends; to appreciate beauty; to find the beauty in others; to leave the world a bit better whether by a healthy child, a garden patch, or a redeemed social condition; to know that one life has breathed easier because you lived here. This is to have succeeded.
—**Ralph Waldo Emerson**

Fret Not | 3

When I look back on all these worries, I remember the story of the old man who said on his deathbed that he had a lot of trouble in his life, most of which never happened.
—**Winston Churchill**

4 | How to Pray According to Jesus

Jesus taught that effective prayer must be:
Unselfish—not alone for oneself.
Believing—according to faith.
Sincere—honest of heart.
Intelligent—according to light.
Trustful—in submission to the Father's all-wise will.
—The Urantia Book, 144:3

5 | Prayer Is Listening

Prayer is not asking.
Prayer is putting oneself in the hands of God,
at his disposition,
and listening to his voice in the depths of our hearts.
—Mother Teresa

6 | Live Long and Prosper

May the whole world enjoy good health,
long life, prosperity,
happiness and peace.
Om, shanti, shanti,
—Vethathiri Maharishi

Finding Contentment in Every Situation | 7

I know what it is to be in need,
and I know what it is to have plenty.
I have learned the secret of being content
in any and every situation,
whether well fed or hungry,
whether living in plenty or in want.
I can do all this through him who gives me strength.
—**Philippians 4:12–13**

Lovingkindness Meditation | 8

May I be happy, well, and peaceful.
May my parents, grandparents, and ancestors be
happy, well,
and peaceful.
May my brothers and sisters, my spouse and children,
my grandchildren,
and all future generations be happy, well, and peaceful.
May all my friends and all my enemies be happy.
May all human beings sharing the earth be happy.
May all forms of life, plants, animals, birds, fish,
and insects be happy.
May all sentient beings in the universe be happy.
May we all be free from suffering and pain.
May we all be free from attachment of greed, anger,
and ignorance.
May we all attain perfect peace and happiness
of Enlightenment through

Buddha's Wisdom and Compassion.
—**Reverend Nakagaki**

9 | Seeking Goodness

I am a woman of valor,
My arms are new with strength.
My hands will plant vineyards;
With dignity will I tend them,
With laughter and with wisdom
will I make them grow;
And I will seek goodness
all the days of my life.
—**Proverbs 31**

10 | You Are Brave

I am whole.
I am learning.
I am letting go.
I am free.
I am talented and courageous.
I am protecting my joy.
I am brave.
I am healing.
I am loving myself.
Unapologetically.
—Alex Elle

There's nothing wrong with being afraid. It's not the
absence of fear, it's overcoming it. Sometimes you've got
to blast through and have faith.
—Emma Watson

Live and Love and Forgive Yourself | 12

I will write a letter to someone I haven't spoken with
for a while.
I will send a message to someone I love dearly.
I will write a poem. I will make art.
I will play my guitar and sing.
I will volunteer myself to help loved ones and friends.
I will eat and drink healthy to show my body
my deep gratitude for its existence and the role
it plays in protecting my soul and spirit.

I will recite my mantras any time I feel
overwhelmed by thoughts that cause anxiety.
I will listen to someone who rarely has
the opportunity to be heard.
I will be aware of my breath and the rhythm of
my heartbeat.

I will laugh and forgive myself when I forget
that I made these promises at the beginning of my day,
and at the end of my day I will celebrate
and congratulate

myself for what I was able to accomplish.
—Julie Henderson

13 | We Are Nurtured by the Same Earth

Out beyond ideas of wrongdoing and rightdoing,
there is a field. I'll meet you there.
When the soul lies down in that grass,
the world is too full to talk about.
Ideas, language, even the phrase "each
other" doesn't make any sense.
—Rumi

14 | Every Single Day Is a Miracle

Each day is a blessing
of epic proportions.
I give thanks for
what might seem meager comforts:
real cream in my coffee,
a day without a bill in the mail...
—Ruth Williams

15 | We Are Only Here to Serve Others

Make us worthy, Lord, to serve our fellow men
throughout the world who live and die in poverty
and hunger.

Give them through our hands this day their daily bread,
and by our understanding love, give peace and joy.
—**Mother Teresa**

Praise Be | 16

Praise, thanksgiving, celebration
and congratulations to God,

The One,
Living, Breathing, Moving,
Active Holy Energy,
Living Spirit,
Creator of the Universe,
of the Oversoul
and of me
and of thee.
—**Luz Antigua**

Our Hearts as Full | 17

To our Gods of old, we bless the ground
that you tread in search of our freedom!
We bless your presence in our lives and in our hearts!
Take of this offering to your delight,
and be filled with our prayers of thanksgiving!
May our lives remain as full as our hearts on this day!
—**Yoruban Chant**

18 | Today Is the Right Day to Love

He said, "There are only two days in the year
that nothing can be done.
One is called yesterday
and the other is called tomorrow,
so today is the right day to love, believe, do and
mostly live."
—Dalai Lama

19 | Everything Will Be All Right

I will breathe.
I will think of solutions.
I will not let my worry control me.
I will not let my stress level break me.
I will simply breathe.
And it will be okay.
Because I don't quit.
—Shayne McClendon

20 | Let There Be Peace and Justice for All Creation

Let us see one another through eyes
enlightened by understanding and compassion.
Release us from judgment so we can receive the stories
of our sisters and brothers with respect and attention.
Open our hearts to the cries of a suffering world

and the healing melodies of peace and justice for
all creation.
Empower us to be instruments of justice
and equality everywhere.
—**Jean Shinoda Bolen, The Millionth Circle**

Lifted | 21

I pray for hope for those who feel none.

I pray for those in despair

to be lifted by the power of love.

I pray we all can be a part

of making this prayer come true.
—**Steve Williamson**

Don't Waste Your Gifts | 22

Feeling gratitude and not expressing it
is like wrapping a present and not giving it.
—**William Arthur Ward**

There Is No Try, Only Do or Do Not | 23

The Bible says not to worry,
so I don't.

I just get up in the morning
and ask God for help to get through the day.
If tomorrow shows up,
then I'll take the same shot tomorrow.
—Paul Henderson

24 | Just Keep Putting One Foot in Front of the Other

You never know what's around the corner.
It could be everything.
Or it could be nothing.
You keep putting one foot in front of the other,
and then one day you look back
and you've climbed a mountain.
—Tom Hiddleston

25 | Take Positive Action

In a time of destruction, create something: a poem, a
parade, a community, a school, a vow, a moral principle;
one peaceful moment.
—Maxine Hong Kingston

26 | Give with an Open Heart

When we give cheerfully and accept gratefully,
everyone is blessed.
—Maya Angelou

Step into the Sunlight
Feel the pain wash away
Enter in the Soul-light
Just BE in today.
Forget all emotion
Put your trust in the day
Let the past rush on by you
Put your Self in THE WAY.
—Lynne Milum

See the Splendor | 28

Shadows bloom and wilt across the patio,
our new home sheds flakes of bright paint,
and, of course, it is October; the neighbors we
don't know
hang pumpkin lights like lamb's blood over
the threshold,
and from their porch rocking chairs stare at us,
the strangers.
We disguise ourselves with smiles and wave.
And why not? Let the leaves fall and the grass grow high,
our new life floats around us in the frost-free air,
and we own the chaos of autumn; the weeds
would grow between our toes if we'd linger
into another two seasons. We are giddy enough
for a picket fence or a pink flamingo
and bring out Baby to see the splendor.
"Here," we say like good parents, "is the color red

and over there, the irrepressible orange of joy."
—Marjorie Maddox

29 | Get in Touch with What Is Real

I'm busy;
but not in the way
most people accept.
I'm busy calming my fear
and finding my courage.
I'm busy listening to my kids.
I'm busy getting in touch
with what is real.
I'm busy growing things and
connecting with the natural world.
I'm busy questioning my answers.
I'm busy being present in my life.
—Brooke Hampton

30 | All You Need to Do Is Be Helpful

I am here only to be truly helpful.
I am here to represent Him Who sent me.
I do not have to worry about what to say or what to do,
because He Who sent me will direct me.
I am content to be wherever He wishes,
knowing He goes there with me.
I will be healed as I let Him teach me to heal.
—*A Course in Miracles*

Harvesting Happiness

"I murmured because I had no shoes, until I met a man
who had no feet."
—**Persian Proverb**

"Gratitude is the inward feeling of kindness received.
Thankfulness is the natural impulse to express that
feeling. Thanksgiving is the following of that impulse."
—**Henry Van Dyke**

"The soul that gives thanks can find comfort in
everything; the soul that complains can find comfort in
nothing."
—**Hannah Whitall Smith**

"Gratitude is like the good faith of traders: it maintains
commerce, and we often pay, not because it is just to
discharge our debts, but that we may more readily find
people to trust us."
— **François de La Rochefoucauld**

"Just as despair can come to one only from other human
beings, hope, too, can be given to one only by other
human beings."
—**Elie Wiesel**

"The thankful receiver bears a plentiful harvest."
—**William Blake**

1 | We Are All Meant to Shine

Our deepest fear is not that we are inadequate. Our
deepest fear is that we are powerful beyond measure.
It is our light, not our darkness that most frightens us.
We ask ourselves, 'Who am I to be brilliant, gorgeous,
talented, fabulous?' Actually, who are you not to be? You
are a child of God. Your playing small does not serve the
world. There is nothing enlightened about shrinking so
that other people won't feel insecure around you. We
are all meant to shine, as children do. We were born to
make manifest the glory of God that is within us. It's
not just in some of us; it's in everyone. And as we let
our own light shine, we unconsciously give other people
permission to do the same. As we are liberated from our
own fear, our presence automatically liberates others.
—**Marianne Williamson**

2 | Healing Touch

Touch the pain of the world
and release hope into the darkness.
—**Sisters of Social Service**

3 | She Weaves the Web of Life

Who is She?
She is your power,
your Feminine source.
Big Mama. The Goddess.

The Great Mystery.
The web-weaver.
The life force.
The first time,
the twentieth time you
may not recognize her.
Or pretend not to hear.
As she fills your body
with ripples of terror and delight.

But when she calls you will know
you've been called.
Then it is up to you to
decide if you will answer.
—**Lucy H. Pearce**

Bless This House | 4

Bless this house, O Lord, we pray,
Make it safe by night and day;
Bless these walls, so firm and stout,
Keeping want and trouble out;
Bless the roof and chimneys tall,
Let thy peace lie over all;
Bless the door, that it may prove
Ever open to joy and love.

Bless these windows shining bright,
Letting in God's heavenly light;
Bless the hearth a-blazing there,
With smoke ascending like a prayer;

Bless the folk who dwell within,
Keep them pure and free from sin;
Bless us all that, one day, we may be
Fit, O Lord, to dwell with Thee...
—Helen Taylor

5 | Start the Day Happy & Kind

Hello, sun in my face.

Hello, you who made the morning and spread it over
the fields.

...

Watch, now, how I start the day

in happiness, in kindness.
—Mary Oliver, from "Why I Wake Early," Devotions

6 | Be Thankful 365, 27/7

Don't pray when it rains
if you don't pray when the sun shines.
—Leroy [Satchel] Paige

7 | New Mercies

Humbly we pray that this mind

may be steadfast in us,
and that through these our hands,
and the hands of others
to whom thou shalt give the same spirit,
thou wilt vouchsafe to endow
the human family with new mercies.
—**Francis Bacon**

Waterfalls of Tenderness | 8

Father, Mother, God,
Thank you for your presence
during the hard and mean days.
For then we have you to lean upon.
Thank you for your presence
during the bright and sunny days,
for then we can share that which we have
with those who have less.
For those who have no voice,
we ask you to speak.
For those who feel unworthy,
we ask you to pour your love out
in waterfalls of tenderness.
—**Maya Angelou**

Lift Your Hands in Prayer | 9

Lord, I cry unto thee: make haste unto me;
give ear unto voice, when I cry unto thee.
Let my prayer be set forth before thee as incense;

and the lifting of my hands as the evening sacrifice.
—**Psalm 141:1–2, King David**

10 | Say Grace

Grace is richer than prayer,
for God always gives more than is asked of him.
—**Ambrose**

11 | Learning Who You Really Are

You may encounter many defeats,
But you must not be defeated.
In fact, it may be necessary
To encounter the defeats,
So you can know who you are,
What you can rise from,
How you can still come out of it.
—**Maya Angelou**

12 | Endue with the Spirit of Wisdom

Almighty God, Who has given us this good land for our
heritage; We humbly beseech Thee that we may always
prove ourselves a people mindful of Thy favor and glad
to do Thy will. Bless our land with honorable ministry,
sound learning, and pure manners.

Save us from violence, discord, and confusion, from
pride and arrogance, and from every evil way. Defend
our liberties, and fashion into one united people
the multitude brought hither out of many kindreds
and tongues.

Endow with Thy spirit of wisdom those to whom in Thy
Name we entrust the authority of government, that there
may be justice and peace at home, and that through
obedience to Thy law, we may show forth Thy praise
among the nations of the earth.

In time of prosperity fill our hearts with thankfulness,
and in the day of trouble, suffer not our trust in Thee
to fail; all of which we ask through Jesus Christ our
Lord, Amen.
—*Book of Common Prayer*

Be Humble and Gentle | 13

Jesus said, "Come to me, all of you
who are weary and carry heavy burdens,
and I will give you rest.
Take my yoke upon you. Let me teach you,
because I am humble and gentle,
and you will find rest for your souls.
For my yoke fits perfectly,
and the burden I give you is light."
—**Matthew 11:28–30, NTL.**

14 | Gladly Received

Bless us, Oh Lord,
and these thy gifts which
we are about to receive from thy bounty,
through Christ, Our Lord.
Amen.
—**Traditional Christian mealtime blessing**

15 | Auspicious Wish

At this very moment, for the peoples and the
nations of the earth,
May not even the names disease, war, famine, and
suffering be heard.
Rather may their moral conduct, merit, wealth, and
prosperity increase,
and may good fortune and well-being always arise
for them.
—**Kyabje Dudjom Rinpoche**

16 | Grant Me Wisdom

I lift these hands, dear God, to You,
in praise and thanks for all you do.
You light the path through all my days
and bless me with your loving ways...

I lift these hands dear God, to You,
in troubled hours when joys are few.

You bear me up on eagles' wings and see
me through each test life brings.

I lift these hands, dear God, to You,
please grant me wisdom, patience, too.
Then fill my heart with love and caring,
precious gifts you've made for sharing.
—**Poet Emily Matthews**

Be a Blessing to Those on Your Way | 17

May your walking be easy, on dry land or snow.
May the good Lord walk with you, wherever you go.
May your troubles brush off, like a sprinkling of dust,
And may you stand strong, for what is good, what is just.

May your soul be always grateful, may joy fill your heart.
May you reach out to others, with love, from the start.
May friendships bring blessing, for you, every day.
And may you be a blessing to those on your way.
—**Blessing, The Rev. Jane R. Dunning**

Don't Question it, Just Give | 18

Great lives belong to men and women
who see life as a generosity contest.
—**Matthew Kelly**

19 | True Beauty

Should you shield the cannons from the windstorms,
you would never see the true beauty of their carvings.
—**Elizabeth Kübler-Ross**

20 | Rest in Him

Remember: Your heart is made to rest in God.
—**Ronald Rolheiser**

21 | Strength and Plenty

A normal day! Holding it in my hand this one last
moment, I have come to see it as more than an ordinary
rock, it is a gem, a jewel. In time of war, in peril of death,
people have dug their hands and faces into the earth and
remembered this. In time of sickness and pain, people
have buried their faces in pillows and wept for this. In
time of loneliness and separation, people have stretched
themselves taut and waited for this. In time of hunger,
homelessness, and wants, people have raised bony hands
to the skies and stayed alive for this.

Normal day, let me be aware of the treasure you are. Let me learn from you, love you, savor you, bless you before you depart. Let me not pass you by in quest of some rare and perfect tomorrow. Let me hold you while I may, for it will not always be so. One day I shall dig my nails into the earth or bury my face in the pillow, or stretch myself taut, or raise my hands to the sky, and want more than all the world your return. And then I will know what now I am guessing: that you are, indeed, a common rock and not a jewel, but that a common rock made of the very mass substance of the earth in all its strength and plenty puts a gem to shame.

—Mary Jean Irion

Moving Prayer | 22

Sometimes it just stuns you
like an arrow flung from some angel's wing.
Sometimes it hastily scribbles
a list in the air: black coffee,
thick new books,
your pillow's cool underside,
the quirky family you married into.

It is content with so little really;
even the ink of your pen along
the watery lines of your dimestore notebook
could be a swiftly moving prayer.

—Andrea Potos

23 | The Sun Will Come Out Tomorrow

Ask Him to remind you when you see a magnificent
sunset that He did that for you.
—Jane Trufant Harvey

24| A Grateful Heart

As each day comes to us refreshed and anew, so does
my gratitude renew itself daily. The breaking of the sun
over the horizon is my grateful heart dawning upon a
blessed world.
—Adabella Radici

25 | Dinner Prayer

God is great. God is good. And we thank Him for our
food. By His hands we must be fed, give us Lord our
daily bread. Amen.
—Traditional Christian mealtime blessing

26 | With a Pure Heart

Help us to love each person because
they are a human being and created in the image of God.

Let not our race, color, religion, or ethnicity be a
dividing factor

but may we see each person as a uniquely created
individual worthy of our love.

Help us to stand against senseless violence and
not support
anyone who would divide others for their own gain.

Make us true instruments of your peace.

In Jesus' Holy name we ask. Amen.
—**Valerie Cullers**

May the Earth Yield Plenty of Corn | 27

May the waters flow peacefully; may the herbs
and plants grow peacefully;
may all the divine powers bring unto us peace.
May the rain come down in the proper time,
may the earth yield plenty of corn,
may the country be free from war.
The supreme Lord is peace.
—**Hindu tradition**

Be a Decent Person | 28

When I lay my head on the pillow at night, I can say I
was a decent person today. That's when I feel beautiful.
—**Drew Barrymore**

29 | Infinite Peace to You

Deep peace of the running wave to you.
Deep peace of the flowing air to you.
Deep peace of the quiet earth to you.
Deep peace of the shining stars to you.
Deep peace of the infinite peace to you.
—**Gaelic Blessing**

30 | Life Is Short, Make the Most of It

Life is like a blink of an eye,
Death is for eternity.
Therefore, life is really just a dream,
And death is the reality.
—**Betty Pritchard**

31 | Be Not Dismayed

Nada te turbe,
Nada te espante,
Toda se pasa,
Dios no se muda,
La Paciencia
Todo la alcanza;
Quien a Dios tiene
Nada le falta,
Sólo Dios basta.

...

Let nothing disturb thee;
Let nothing dismay thee;
All things pass:
God never changes.
Patience attains
All that it strives for.
He who has God
Lacks for nothing:
God alone suffices.
—**St. Teresa of Avila**

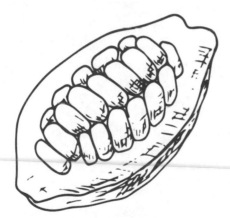

NOVEMBER

Sharing Thanksgiving and Togetherness

"Gratitude and esteem are good foundations of affection."
—**Jane Austen**

"Be happy, noble heart, be blessed for all the good thou hast done and wilt do hereafter, and let my gratitude remain in obscurity like your good deeds."
—**Alexandre Dumas**

"The worship most acceptable to God comes from a thankful and cheerful heart."
—**Plutarch**

"We should always pray for help, but we should always listen for inspiration and impression to proceed in ways different from those we may have thought of."
—**John H. Groberg**

"Gratitude is the fairest blossom which springs from the soul."
—**Henry Ward Beecher**

Thankfulness Defined | 1

Gratitude (noun): The quality of being thankful;
readiness to show appreciation for and to
return kindness; gratefulness, thankfulness,
thanks, appreciation, indebtedness; recognition,
acknowledgment, credit.
—**Mary Anne Radmacher**

Two Words of Gratitude | 2

Within the context of everything you do, pause—really
slow down—and say thank you. Look at the checker in
the eye, take a breath, and say, "thank you." Pause before
a meal and give thanks to the farmers and the earth and
the animals or the Coca-Cola distributor who brought
the food to your table. Say, "thank you."
—**Polly Campbell**

Domo Arigato | 3

A globetrotting friend of mine told me that the first
thing she would do before setting foot in another
country was learn how to say, "Thank you," and the
native tongue. "You'd be surprised at the delight others
take in hearing a foreigner's tongue speak their own
language," she said. "They were sometimes surprised,
other times impressed, and sometimes they would have
no idea what I was saying! But they were always grateful
for my attempts."

Here's a list of the world's many ways to express
your gratitude:

Arabic: Shukran
Czech: D kuji
Danish: Tak
Dutch: Dank u
Estonian: Tanan teid
Filipino: Salamat
Finnish: Kiitos
French: Merci
Gaelic: Go raibh maith agat
German: Danke
Hungarian: Koszonom
Indonesian: Terima Kasih
Italian: Grazie
Japanese: Arigato
Latvian: Paldies
Norwegian: Takk
Polish: Dzi kuj
Portuguese: Obrigado
Romanian: Mul umesc
Spanish: Gracias
Swahili: Asante
Swedish: Tack
Vietnamese: Cam on ban
Welsh: Diolch yn fawr
—Brenda Knight

Learn to let go. That is the key to happiness.
—**Buddah**

The Abundant Vow | 5

The food comes from the Earth and the Sky,
It is the gift of the entire universe
And the fruit of much hard work;
I vow to live a life which is worthy of receiving it.
—**Grace of the Bodhisattva Buddhists**

As This Food Restores Our Soul | 6

May this food restore our strength,
giving new energy to tired limbs,
new thoughts to weary minds.

May this drink restore our souls,
giving new vision to dry spirits,
new warmth to cold hearts.

And once refreshed,
may we give new pleasure to you,
who gives us all.
Amen.
—**Author Unknown**

7 | Prayer to St. Joseph the Protector

O St. Joseph whose protection is so great, so strong,
so prompt before the Throne of God,
I place in you all my interests and desires.
O St. Joseph do assist me by your powerful intercession
and obtain for me from your Divine Son
all spiritual blessings through Jesus Christ, Our Lord;
so that having engaged here below your Heavenly power
I may offer my Thanksgiving and Homage
to the most Loving of Fathers.
O St. Joseph, I never weary contemplating you
and Jesus asleep in your arms.
I dare not approach while He reposes near your heart.
Press him in my name and kiss His fine Head for me,
and ask Him to return the Kiss when I draw my
dying breath.
St. Joseph, Patron of departing souls,
pray for us.
Amen...
—**Prayer to St. Joseph**

8 | I Give Thanks for the Joys

I Receive ALL of Life with Thanksgiving
I have gratitude for EVERYTHING
that has ever occurred to bring me to this moment.
I give thanks for the joys and the sufferings,
the moments of peace and the flashes of anger,
the compassion and the indifference,
the roar of my courage and the cold sweat of my fear.

I accept gratefully the entirety of my past and my
present life.
—**Jonathan Lockwood Huie**

Surround Yourself with Gratitude | 9

It's no secret that practicing gratitude as a daily ritual
requires your brain to see the cup half full. You'll be
happier, healthier, and more grateful for the blessings in
your life.

Have you ever noticed the way it feels to be around
grateful people? You feel energized, alive, and inspired
to give thanks yourself for the friends, families, and
community members that make a difference in your
daily life. When we're grateful, we reach out to help
others in need, instead of focusing on our own woes,
anger, or resentments.
—**Nina Lesowitz**

The Virtue of Patience | 10

Thank you for your life of perfect patience,
lived in my place.
Give me strength today
to reflect your patience to others.
Amen.
—**Mollie Schairer**

11 | In Stillness, You Can Hear God

I speak to you through the mysterious rainbow.
Be still
Know I am God.

I will speak to you when you are alone
Be still
Know I am God.

I will speak to you through the Wisdom of the Ancients.
Be still
Know I am God.

I will speak to you at the end of time.
Be still
Know I am God.

I will speak to you when you have seen my Angels.
Be still
Know I am God.

I will speak to you throughout Eternity.
Be still
Know I am God.

I speak to you.
Be still
Know I am God.
—**Essene Gospel of Peace**

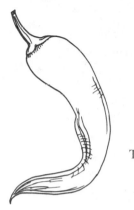

Shine Your Love Down | 12

All the cattle are resting in the fields,
The trees and the plants are growing,
The birds flutter above the marshes,
Their wings uplifted in adoration,
And all the sheep are dancing,
All winged things are flying,
They live when you have shone on them.
—**Ancient Egyptian Ode to the Sun**

In Your Hands | 13

I thank you, O God, for your care and protection this
day, keeping me from physical harm and spiritual
corruption. I now place the work of the day into your
hands, trusting that you will redeem my errors and turn
my achievements to your glory. And I now ask you to
work within me, trusting that you will use the hours of
rest to create in me a new heart and new soul.
—**Jacob Boehme**

Don't Waste a Moment | 14

This new day is too dear,
with its hopes and invitations,
to waste a moment on the rotten yesterdays.
—**Ralph Waldo Emerson**

15 | Life's Big Questions

Take out your journal and a pen and set aside twenty minutes for this exercise in thankfulness.

Gratitude is the surest way to heal your heart and soul and to move your focus to what is good and working in your life. It's also the fastest way, I've found, to make a difference in your day. When we commit to a regular gratitude practice, we start to see the webs of meaning sticking to all the crannies in our lives and we find even more reasons to be grateful for all that we have.

For example, when I lost four magazine assignments, and all of my income, in a twenty-four-hour period, I got nervous, then I freaked. Then, after a few deep breaths, I got curious and stated asking The Big Questions: What is the meaning behind this? What can I do with this? What is working?

The answers to those questions helped me to get clear about my situation and helped me to recognize all that I did have to be grateful for (a husband with a job, a little money in the bank, breath in my lungs, and mint chocolate chip in the freezer).

From that place of gratitude, I could start seeing the possibilities the lost work provided. It freed up my schedule to follow a dream I'd had for decades-the writing of this book. When I gave thanks for my life as it was, I could see the meaning behind the lost assignments, and a dismal situation became a lie-changing experience.

Now, you try it. In this exercise you'll have a chance to begin a practice of gratitude and find those gifts of meaning in your own life.

1. List ten things you are thankful for.
2. How many of those things evolved out of less than perfect circumstances?
3. Pick one to write about. Describe how it came to be in your life.
4. What did you learn from it?
5. What did you do as a result of it?
6. What meaning does it hold for you?

—Polly Campbell

My Cup Overflows | 16

The Lord is my shepherd, I lack nothing. He makes me lie down in green pastures, he leads me beside quiet waters, he refreshes my soul. He guides me along the right paths for his name's sake. Even though I walk through the darkest valley, I will fear no evil, for you are with me; your rod and your staff, they comfort me. You prepare a table before me in the presence of my enemies. You anoint my head with oil; my cup overflows. Surely your goodness and love will follow me all the days of my life and I will dwell in the house of the Lord forever.

—Psalm 23:1–6

17 | Thank You

Thank you God for the world so sweet,
Thank you God for the food we eat.
Thank you God for the birds that sing,
Thank you God for everything.
—**Christian Children's Prayer**

18 | Every Forest Is a Calendar

& what if hope crashes through the door what if

that lasts a somersault?

hope for serendipity

even if a series of meals were all between us

even if the aeons lined up out

of order

what are years if not measured by trees?
—**"Elegy," by Mong-Lan**

19 | How Often Do You Say Thank You?

Your Beliefs
Your attitude
Your thoughts

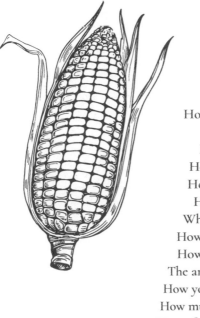

Your perspective
How honest you are
Who your friends are
What books you read
How often you exercise
The type of food you eat
How many risks you take
How you interpret the situation
How kind you are to others
How kind you are to yourself
How often you say "I love you."
How often you say "thank you."
How you express your feelings
Whether or not you ask for help
How often you practice gratitude
How many times you smile today
The amount of effort you put forth
How you spend / invest your money
How much time you spend worrying
How often you think about your past
Whether or not you judge other people
Whether or not you try again after a setback
How much you appreciate the things you have
—Caleb LP Gunner

NOVEMBER

Keep It Simple | 20

If the only prayer you say in your life is thank you,
that would suffice.
—**Meister Eckhart**

21 | Reduced to Joy

"There is a calmness to a life lived in gratitude,
a quiet joy."
—Ralph H. Blum

22 | Let Us Proclaim Our Gratitude

Let us therefore proclaim our gratitude to Providence
for manifold blessings—let us be humbly thankful
for inherited ideals—and let us resolve to share those
blessings and those ideals with our fellow human beings
throughout the world.

...

On that (this) day let us gather in sanctuaries dedicated
to worship and in homes blessed by family affection to
express our gratitude for the glorious gifts of God; and
let us earnestly and humbly pray that He will continue
to guide and sustain us in the great unfinished tasks of
achieving peace, justice, and understanding among all
men and nations and of ending misery and suffering
wherever they exist.
—President John F. Kennedy

23 | Stay on Purpose

Thank you, God, for food so good,
and help us do the things we should.

Help us with our work and play,
and everything we do and say.
Amen.
—**Author Unknown**

Life Is Good | 24

When you are feeling down
And all you can muster up is a frown
That is the time to stop
And count your blessings until you drop.

Focus on all of life's good
And you will find things work out as they should
Feeling sorry and just sitting around
It is a sure thing to bring you down.

Take some action, make a move
It doesn't matter if others approve
Nothing lasts forever
You will move past this if you endeavor!
—**Catherine Pulsifer**

The Bright Side of Life | 25

Gratitude can transform common days into
thanksgivings, turn routine jobs into joy, and change
ordinary opportunities into blessings.
—**William Arthur Ward**

26 | The Earth Is Just So Full of Fun

It's all a farce,—these tales they tell
About the breezes sighing,
And moans astir o'er field and dell,
Because the year is dying.

Such principles are most absurd,—
I care not who first taught 'em;
There's nothing known to beast or bird
To make a solemn autumn.

In solemn times, when grief holds sway
With countenance distressing,
You'll note the more of black and gray
Will then be used in dressing.

Now purple tints are all around;
The sky is blue and mellow;
And e'en the grasses turn the ground
From modest green to yellow.

The seed burrs all with laughter crack
On featherweed and jimson;
And leaves that should be dressed in black
Are all decked out in crimson.

A butterfly goes winging by;
A singing bird comes after;
And Nature, all from earth to sky,
Is bubbling o'er with laughter.

The ripples wimple on the rills,
Like sparkling little lasses;
The sunlight runs along the hills,
And laughs among the grasses.

The earth is just so full of fun
It really can't contain it;
And streams of mirth so freely run
The heavens seem to rain it.

Don't talk to me of solemn days
In autumn's time of splendor,
Because the sun shows fewer rays,
And these grow slant and slender.

Why, it's the climax of the year,—
The highest time of living!—
Till naturally its bursting cheer
Just melts into thanksgiving.
—**Paul Laurence Dunbar**

Drink in Every Moment | 27

The best way to pay for a lovely moment is to enjoy it.
—**Richard Bach**

Peace, Equality, Inclusion for All | 28

May those without voice be heard. May those without
food be fed.

May those who are harmed be healed. May the earth's health be restored. May all have peace, equality, inclusion for all.
—**Alycia Longriver Davis**

29 | Thanks for Your Love

Oludumare, oh Divine One! I give thanks to You, the one who is as near as my heartbeat, and more anticipated than my next breath. Let Your wisdom become one with this vessel as I lift my voice in thanks for Your love.
—**Yoruban Chant**

30 | Mi Sheberakh; May the One Who Blessed

May the One who blessed our ancestors—
Patriarchs Abraham, Isaac, and Jacob,
Matriarchs Sarah, Rebecca, Rachel, and Leah—
bless and heal the one who is ill:
(name) son/daughter of (name).
May the Holy Blessed One
overflow with compassion upon him/her,
to restore him/her,
to heal him/her,
to strengthen him/her,
to enliven him/her.
The One will send him/her, speedily,

a complete healing—
healing of the soul and healing of the body—
along with all the ill,
among the people of Israel and all humankind,
soon,
speedily,
without delay,
and let us all say:
Amen.
—Traditional Jewish Prayer for the Sick

DECEMBER

Celebrating What We Have with Those We Love

"Appreciation can change a day, even change a life. Your willingness to put it into words is all that is necessary."
—**Margaret Cousins**

"Religion is grace and ethics is gratitude."
—**Thomas Erskine**

"Faith is taking the first step even when you don't see the whole staircase."
—**Martin Luther King Jr.**

"The poor man shuddered, overflowed with an angelic joy; he declared in his transport that this would last through life; he said to himself that he really had not suffered enough to deserve such radiant happiness, and he thanked God, in the depths of his soul, for having permitted that he, a miserable man, should be so loved."
—**Victor Hugo**

"Do not spoil what you have by desiring what you have not; remember that what you now have was once among the things you only hoped for."
—**Epicurus**

Thank You God for This Most Amazing Morning | 1

i thank You God for most this amazing
day: for the leaping greenly spirits of trees
and a blue true dream of sky; and for everything
which is natural which is infinite which is yes

(i who have died am alive again today,
and this is the sun's birthday; this is the birth
day of life and of love and wings: and of the gay
great happening illimitably earth)

how should tasting touching hearing seeing
breathing any—lifted from the no
of all nothing—human merely being
doubt unimaginable You?

(now the ears of my ears awake and
now the eyes of my eyes are opened)
—E. E. Cummings

I Say a Little Prayer for You | 2

Grace isn't a little prayer you chant before receiving a
meal. It's a way to live.
—Attributed to Jacqueline Winspear

3 | It All Comes from the Same Source

I go into
the Muslim mosque
and the Jewish synagogue
and the Christian church
and I see one
altar.
—**Allen Ginsberg**

4 | Seasons of the Soul

The world is not imperfect or slowly evolving along a
path to perfection. No, it is perfect at every moment,
every sin already carries grace in it.
—**Hermann Hesse**

5 | Pay Attention

The Sustainer of
our bodies, hearts, and souls,
Bless all
that we thankfully
receive.
Amen.
—**Pir-o-Murshid Hazrat Inayat Khan**

Walk Humbly with My God | 6

Rabbi Jesus the Messiah teaches me
to live fully
to act justly
to love tenderly
to walk humbly with my God and
where necessary to lose graciously.
—**Alan Kaufman**

Today Is God | 7

In the beginning was God,
Today is God,
Tomorrow will be God.
Who can make an image of God?
He has no body.
He is the word which comes out of your mouth.
That word!
It is no more,
It is past, and still it lives!
So is God.
—**African Tribal Pygmy Prayer**

Your Life Is a Prayer | 8

When I am liberated by silence,
when I am no longer involved
in the measurement of life, but in the living of it,
I can discover a form of prayer in which

there is effectively no distraction.
My whole life becomes a prayer.
My whole silence is full of prayer.
The world of silence in which I am immersed
contributes to my prayer.
—**Thomas Merton**

9 | Love Eternal

O Give thanks unto the Lord;
for he is good:
for his mercy endureth forever.
—**Psalm 118:1, KJV**

10 | Rain Brings Flowers

If you want the rainbow,
you have to put up with the rain.
—**Dolly Parton**

11 | It's What You Do with What You are Handed

The question
for each man to settle
is not what he would do if he had
means, time, influence, and educational advantages,
but what he will do with the things he has.
—**Hamilton Wright Mabie**

Today Is Sweet | 12

Ah, Fill the cup—
What boots it to repeat
How time is slipping underneath our feet,
Unborn Tomorrow,
And dead Yesterday
Why fret about them
If Today be sweet!!
—**Omar Khayyam**

The Fullness of Life | 13

Let each day be so fashioned as though
it were closing the line of days
and completely fulfilling life.
If then God grants us the morrow,
let us accept it with a happy heart.
—**Seneca**

Own Your True Self. Fully. | 14

There's something liberating about not pretending.
Dare to embarrass yourself. Risk.
—**Drew Barrymore**

Peace on Your House | 15

If there is to be peace in the world,

There must be peace in the nations.
If there is to be peace in the nations,
There must be peace in the cities.
If there is to be peace in the cities,
There must be peace between neighbors.
If there is to be peace between neighbors,
There must be peace in the home.
If there is to be peace in the home,
There must be peace in the heart.
—Lao Tzu

16 | Passing Right through the Gates of Heaven

Blessed are they who give
without expecting even thanks in return,
for they shall be abundantly rewarded.

...

Blessed are they who love and trust their fellow
beings,
for they shall reach the good in people and
receive a loving response.

...

Blessed are they who after dedicating their lives
and thereby receiving a blessing, have the courage
and faith
to surmount the difficulties of the path ahead,

for they shall receive a second blessing.

Blessed are they who advance toward the spiritual
path
without the selfish motive of seeking inner peace,
for they shall find it.

Blessed are they who instead of trying to
batter down the gates of the kingdom of heaven
approach them humbly and lovingly and purified,
for they shall pass right through.
—**Peace Pilgrim**

Splendors of the Dayspring | 17

I have awakened in Thy shelter, O my God,
and it becometh him that seeketh that shelter
to abide within the Sanctuary of Thy Protection
and the Stronghold of Thy defense.
Illumine my inner being, O my Lord,
with the splendors of the Dayspring of Thy Revelation,
even as Thou didst illumine my outer being
with the morning light of Thy favor.
—**Bahá'u'lláh**

18 | Anywhere Can Be the Happiest Place on Earth

Remember you're the one who can fill the world with sunshine.
—**Snow White,** *Snow White and the Seven Dwarfs*

19 | The Sweetest Hope

Hope is the thing with feathers
That perches in the soul,
And sings the tune without the words,
And never stops at all,

And sweetest in the gale is heard;
And sore must be the storm
That could abash the little bird
That kept so many warm.

I've heard it in the chillest land,
And on the strangest sea;
Yet, never, in extremity,
It asked a crumb of me.
—**Emily Dickinson**

20 | Heaven Can Be a Place on Earth

Dance as though no one is watching you,
Love as though you have never been hurt before,
Sing as though no one can hear you,

Live as though heaven is on earth.
—**Susanna Clark and Richard Leigh**

Spread Cheer Every Chance You Get | 21

After every storm, the sun will smile;
for every problem, there is a solution,
and the soul's indefeasible duty is to be of good cheer.
—**William R. Alger**

A December Blessings | 22

Let there be respect for the earth, Peace for its people,
Love in our lives,
Delight in the good, Forgiveness for past wrongs and
from now on, a new start.
—**Reverend Peter Trow**

Wherever I Am, God Is | 23

The light of God surrounds me;
The love of God enfolds me;
The power of God protects me;
The presence of God watches over me.
Wherever I am, God is.
—**James Dillet Freeman**

24 | Empty Your Heart of Fears

Do you need Me?
I am there.
You cannot see Me, yet I am the light you see by.
You cannot hear Me, yet I speak through your voice.
You cannot feel Me, yet I am the power at work in
your hands.
I am at work, though you do not understand My ways.
I am at work, though you do not understand My works.
I am not strange visions. I am not mysteries.
Only in absolute stillness, beyond self, can you know Me
as I am, and then but as a feeling and a faith.
Yet I am there. Yet I hear. Yet I answer.
When you need Me, I am there.
Even if you deny Me, I am there.
Even when you feel most alone, I am there.
Even in your fears, I am there.
Even in your pain, I am there.
I am there when you pray and when you do not pray.
I am in you, and you are in Me.
Only in your mind can you feel separate from Me, for
only in your mind are the mists of "yours" and "mine."
Yet only with your mind can you know Me and
experience Me.
Empty your heart of empty fears.
When you get yourself out of the way, I am there
You can of yourself do nothing, but I can do all.
And I am in all.
Though you may not see the good, good is there, for
I am there. I am there because I have to be, because I am.
Only in Me does the world have meaning;

only out of Me does the world take form;
only because of Me does the world go forward.
I am the law on which the movement of the stars
and the growth of living cells are founded.
I am the love that is the law's fulfilling.
I am assurance.
I am peace.
I am oneness.
I am the law that you can live by.
I am the love that you can cling to.
I am your assurance.
I am your peace.
I am ONE with you.
I am.
Though you fail to find Me, I do not fail you.
Though your faith in Me is unsure,
My faith in you never wavers,
because I know you, because I love you.
Beloved, I AM there.
—James Dillet Freeman

Pray About Everything | 25

Always be full of joy in the Lord.
I say it again—rejoice!
Let everyone see that you are considerate in all you do.
Remember the Lord is coming soon.
Don't worry about anything,
instead pray about everything.
Tell God what you need,
and thank him for all he has done.

If you do this, you will experience God's peace,
which is far more wonderful
than the human mind can understand.
His peace will guard your hearts and minds
as you live in Christ Jesus.
—Philippians 4:4–7, NLT

26 | Be Still until the Sunlight Pours Through

Go forward with courage. When you are in doubt, be still, and wait; when doubt no longer exists for you, then go forward with courage. So long as mists envelop you, be still; be still until the sunlight pours through and dispels the mists—as it surely will. Then act with courage.
—Chief White Eagle, Ponca Chief

27 | There Is Plenty Enough for All

May all be fed. May all be healed. May all be loved.
—John Robbins

Everything You Need Is within You | 28

It was when I stopped searching for home within others
and lifted the foundations of home within myself I found
there were no roots more intimate than those between a
mind and body that have decided to be whole.
—Rupi Kaur

Miraculous Scope of Human Generosity | 29

In the end, though, maybe we must all give up trying
to pay back the people in this world who sustain our
lives. In the end, maybe it's wiser to surrender before the
miraculous scope of human generosity and to just keep
saying thank you, forever and sincerely, for as long as we
have voices.
—Elizabeth Gilbert

Practice Kindness | 30

Beginning today, treat everyone you meet as if they were
going to be dead by midnight. Extend to them all the
care, kindness and understanding you can muster, and do
it with no thought of any reward. Your life will never be
the same again.
—Og Mandino

31 | Joy for the Coming Year

If we are ever to enjoy life, now is the time–not
tomorrow, nor next year, nor in some future life after we
have died. The best preparation for a better life next year
is a full, complete, harmonious, joyous life this year. Our
beliefs in a rich future life are of little importance unless
we coin them into a rich present life. Today should
always be our most wonderful day.
—**Thomas Dreier**

Be Thankful *For* Each Other, Be Thankful Together

In closing, we thought we would share with you one last way that you can express all of this newfound gratitude, and that is by opening up a "Gratitude Circle." The idea is simple: A gratitude circle is a place for sharing stories, photos, prayers of gratitude, and videos with friends and loved ones. The more people you can get to align with you, the sooner you will discover the positive power of gratitude and reap the many benefits that come from doing so. We want to spread that gift and help you become cheerleaders for others who have tapped into the power of thankfulness by forming your own Gratitude Circle.

By creating a Gratitude Circle, you can join us in being grateful. Connect with others in this special group that's dedicated to honoring the simple phrases "Thank you" and "I am grateful for…". We know firsthand that once you start a thankfulness circle, it won't take long for others to join in, and the power of gratefulness will permeate and bless your everyday being.

There are several ways you can take part in a Gratitude Circle or even create your own Gratitude Group. We make it easy for you with our tips for starting a circle.

Opening to Thankfulness

1. As the organizer of the Gratitude Circle, consider yourself the host or hostess, almost as if you have invited a group of friends—or people with which you hope to become friends—to your dinner table. Your role is to help guide conversations and serve up a feast (of interesting stories about gratitude or nuggets of information to share) that will keep the conversations meaningful and inspiring, ultimately bringing to life the power of gratitude in all the lives of those gathered in your circle.

2. Create a Mission or Goals for your Gratitude Circle. What do you want to accomplish? How will you manifest gratitude in your own life and in the lives of those in your circle? Will you share stories, inspiring quotes, or guided meditations? Create a plan for guiding your group through the practice of gratitude.

3. Decide Whether to Meet Online or In Person—Stay Healthy! The exciting thing about the internet is that you can create a Gratitude Circle and community online, connecting with friends and colleagues from across the country—and the world.

4. Send out e-vites, invites, and make phone calls to invite members to your Gratitude Circle. Ask everyone to invite a friend and spread the word about your new group.

5. Select a meet-up place. Often guides will invite in-person communities to meet at their home. You may opt for a local coffee shop or a comfortable meeting place where you can gather regularly.

6. Create a calendar of meet-up dates and distribute it to your group.

7. Spread the good news about what being thankful can do as it manifests in your life and in the lives of your friends, family, and members of your Gratitude Circle.

The Healing Power of Gratitude

Those simple suggestions should help you get your Gratitude Circle started. Remember, nothing is cast in stone—feel free to improvise until you find your comfort zone. We guarantee you will come away from these gatherings feeling inspired, challenged, and excited to share new ideas. For the most part, this also works very well on Zoom!

First, begin by welcoming your guests. Go around the circle and have each person introduce themselves. For example, "I am Mary Smith and I live in Ohio. I am a writer, literacy volunteer, and mother of two." Next, read a passage of poetry, prayer, or prose. We recommend sections of either the Introduction or the beginning of Chapter Two of this workbook. Now, go clockwise around the circle and ask each participant why they are here and what spiritual sustenance they are seeking.

Ask a volunteer to read their favorite prayer or quote about being thankful. These group gatherings are wonderful, but personal sharing and goal discussion can be intimidating at first, so be mindful of your group and you'll sense when you will need to wrap things up. Always end on a high note by asking each person to share gratitude. May your transformation be your inspiration!

C
O
N
C
L
U
S
I
O
N

ABOUT THE AUTHOR

Becca Anderson comes from a long line of preachers and teachers from Ohio and Kentucky. The teacher side of her family led her to become a woman's studies scholar and the author of *The Book of Awesome Women*. An avid collector of meditations, prayers and blessings, she helps run a "Gratitude and Grace Circle" that meets monthly at homes, churches, and bookstores (also on Zoom during challenging times!) in the San Francisco Bay Area where she currently resides. Becca Anderson credits her spiritual practice with helping her recover from cancer and wants to share this with anyone who is facing difficulty in their life.

Author of *Prayers for Calm* and *Every Day Thankful*, Becca Anderson shares her inspirational writings and suggested acts of kindness at thedailyinspoblog.wordpress.com/

Mango Publishing, established in 2014, publishes an eclectic list of books by diverse authors—both new and established voices—on topics ranging from business, personal growth, women's empowerment, LGBTQ studies, health, and spirituality to history, popular culture, time management, decluttering, lifestyle, mental wellness, aging, and sustainable living. We were recently named 2019 *and* 2020's #1 fastest-growing independent publisher by *Publishers Weekly*. Our success is driven by our main goal, which is to publish high-quality books that will entertain readers as well as make a positive difference in their lives.

Our readers are our most important resource; we value your input, suggestions, and ideas. We'd love to hear from you—after all, we are publishing books for you!

Please stay in touch with us and follow us at:

Facebook: Mango Publishing
Twitter: @MangoPublishing
Instagram: @MangoPublishing
LinkedIn: Mango Publishing
Pinterest: Mango Publishing
Newsletter: mangopublishinggroup.com/newsletter

Join us on Mango's journey to reinvent publishing, one book at a time.